AF575413

PAOLO VENEZIANO'S
CORONATION OF THE VIRGIN

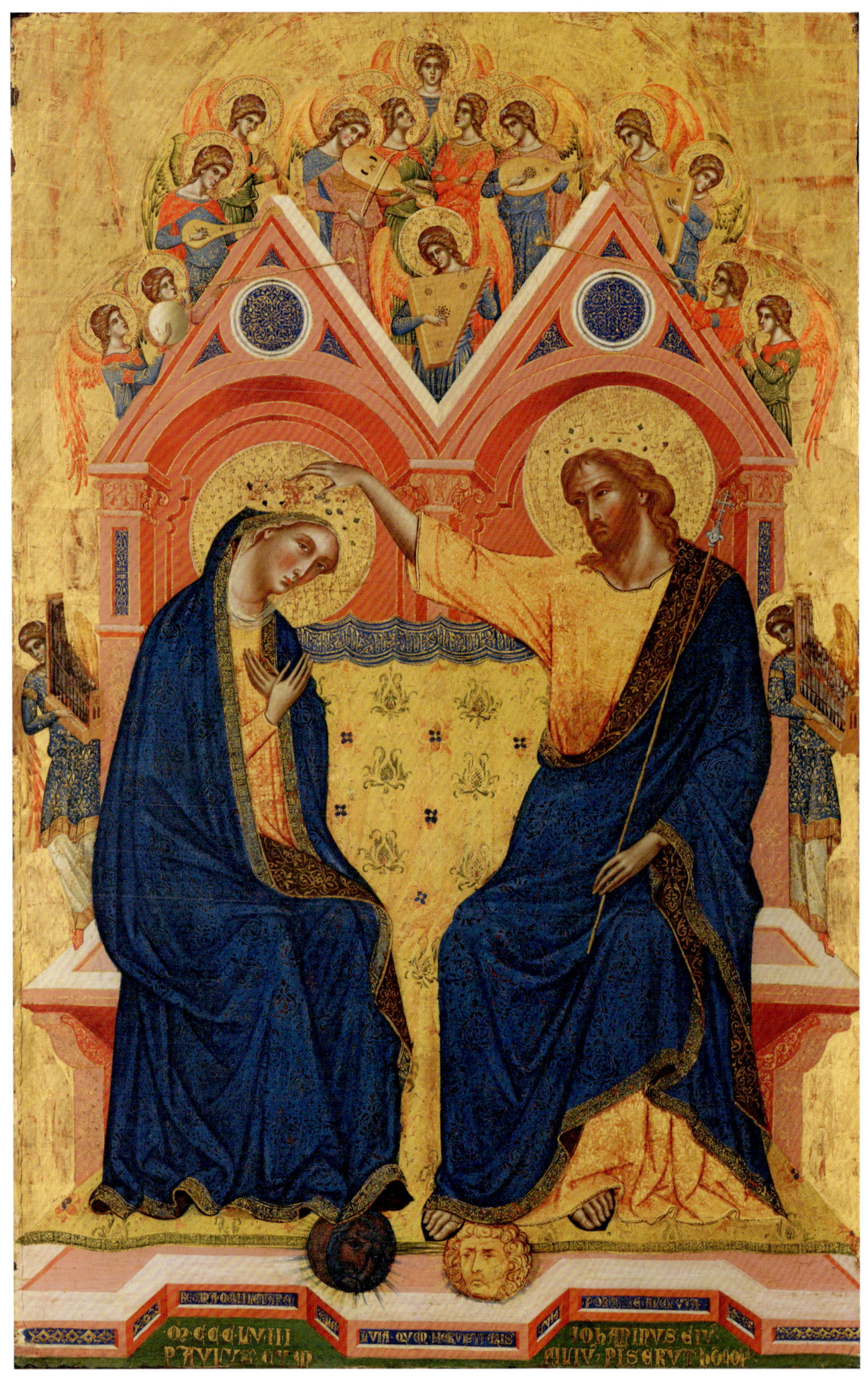

M·C·C·C·LVIII

PAOLO VENEZIANO'S CORONATION OF THE VIRGIN

Nico Muhly

Xavier F. Salomon

The Frick Collection
in association with D Giles Limited

g

FRICK DIPTYCH SERIES

Designed to foster critical engagement and interest specialist and non-specialist alike, each book in this series illuminates a single work in the Frick's rich collection with an essay by a Frick curator paired with a contribution from a contemporary artist or writer.

First published in 2022 by The Frick Collection
1 East 70th Street
New York, NY 10021
www.frick.org

Michaelyn Mitchell, Editor in Chief
Christopher Snow Hopkins, Assistant Editor

In association with GILES
An imprint of D Giles Limited
66 High Street
Lewes, BN7 1XG, UK
gilesltd.com

Copyedited and proofread by Sarah Kane
Designed by Caroline and Roger Hillier,
The Old Chapel Graphic Design

Produced by GILES

Printed and bound in China

A CIP catalogue record for this book is available from the Library of Congress.

ISBN 978-1-913875-15-2

Cover and pages 6, 10, 18, 68, 73, and 78: details from Paolo Veneziano with Giovanni Veneziano, *The Coronation of the Virgin* (frontispiece)

Frontispiece: Paolo Veneziano with Giovanni Veneziano, *The Coronation of the Virgin*, 1358. Tempera on panel, 43¼ x 27 in. (109.9 x 68.6 cm). The Frick Collection, New York

CONTENTS

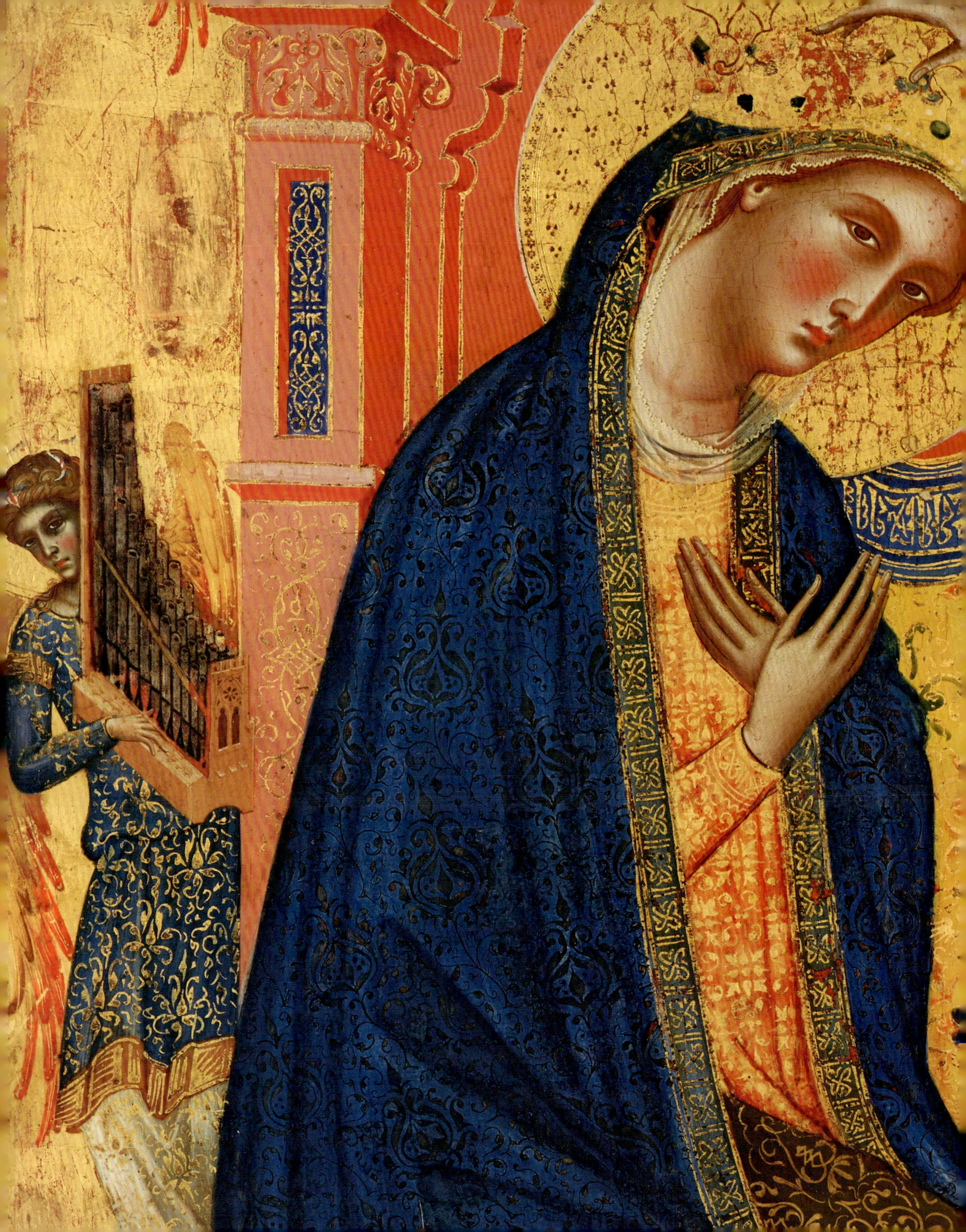

DIRECTOR'S FOREWORD

Historically lauded as the father of Venetian painting, Paolo Veneziano (ca. 1295–ca. 1362) achieved great success as the master of a renowned workshop in Venice. Long thought to be an independent work but now known to be part of a large altarpiece, Paolo's stunning *Coronation of the Virgin*—executed with the assistance of his son Giovanni—is considered the most important of this artist's few works in American museums. With its worked gold surfaces, brilliant palette, and iconographic complexity, the panel is an innovative fusion of traditions from Byzantium and other artistic centers and a most deserving subject of the close look given it in this, the eighth volume in the Frick's Diptych series.

Xavier F. Salomon, the Frick's Deputy Director and Peter Jay Sharp Chief Curator, colorfully sets the scene with an engrossing picture of the eventful times in which Paolo worked and prospered—which included the devastating Black Death—then presents a thorough discussion of what is known of his life and work. As Paolo's panel is surmounted by a retinue of sixteen angels playing instruments, it is only fitting that Xavier's essay be paired with a text by composer Nico Muhly, who describes *The Coronation of the Virgin* as "a panel of pure theater and music." The insightful perspectives they bring to the subject complement each other and harmonize with the divine music of this majestic work of art. We are deeply grateful to them both.

Others to whom thanks are due include Editor in Chief Michaelyn Mitchell, who managed the production of the publication and, with Assistant Editor Christopher Snow Hopkins, edited the texts; and Curatorial Assistant Rebecca Leonard. Finally, we would also like to acknowledge our publishing partner D Giles Limited.

Ian Wardropper
Anna-Maria and Stephen Kellen Director, The Frick Collection

ACKNOWLEDGMENTS

As I charted the waters of Trecento Venice in this journey to the origins of Venetian painting, I was lucky to have been accompanied by many colleagues and friends. At the Frick, I would like to thank Ian Wardropper, Anna-Maria and Stephen Kellen Director, and the Board of Trustees for their unwavering support of research by the Curatorial Department. My fellow curators—Marie-Laure Buku Pongo, Giulio Dalvit, and Aimee Ng—are always a source of inspiration and have been my companions for many conversations around the topic of Paolo Veneziano, and much more besides. Michaelyn Mitchell oversees production and, with Christopher Snow Hopkins, always beautifully works her editing magic on my texts. Rebecca Leonard has been an invaluable assistant, as always, especially in aiding with my research and assembling the images for this book. Joe Godla has provided the reconstructions of the San Severino Polyptych, and I am grateful for many discussions with him on the subject. I would also like to thank Sally Brazil, Susan Chore, Joe Coscia, Julia Day, Bailey Keiger, Julie Ludwig, Gemma McElroy, Jenna Nugent, and Gianna Puzzo.

Nico Muhly has provided the most stimulating essay for this book, and it has been a privilege to work with him on this project. Thanks to him I will never "listen" to Paolo Veneziano's *Coronation* in the same way.

It is an honor to serve on the board of Save Venice and to have been able to follow, thanks to the sponsorship of this great institution, the restoration of the Santa Chiara Polyptych over the past three years. I would like to thank, in particular, Christopher Apostle, Claire Barry, Patricia Fortini Brown, Chris Christner, Melissa Conn, Leslie Contarini, Tracy Cooper, Brendan Davey, C. D. Dickerson, Ferigo Foscari, Amy Gross, Anne Hawley, Frederick Ilchman, Sarah McHam, Alberto Nardi, Laura Sico, Kimberly Tamboer, Irina Tolstoy, and Tina Walls. At the Misericordia Laboratory in Venice, Giulio Manieri Elia and Valeria Poletto were generous hosts along with the restoration team who worked on the painting: Roberto Saccuman and Milena Dean.

Roberto Saccuman has been a wonderful interlocutor for discussing the possibilities of reconstructing the San Severino Polyptych. I would also like to thank George Bisacca, for traveling to San Severino with me to examine the panels by Paolo Veneziano there.

I learned a lot from the art historians who have worked so exceptionally on Paolo Veneziano in the past and continue to do so, in particular Andrea De Marchi and Cristina Guarnieri. A thank you, as always, to Keith Christiansen, for making me think of art in such a rich and wonderful way. Laura Llewellyn and John Witty taught me a huge amount about Paolo Veneziano through their exhibition on the artist in Los Angeles in 2021 and its accompanying catalogue. A particular thank you to John, who accompanied me on a memorable trip to Venice, the Veneto, Croatia, and the Marche in the footsteps of Paolo, in the summer of 2018.

In San Severino Marche, I would like to express my gratitude to the Mayor, Rosa Piermattei, and the Assessore alla Cultura, Vanna Bianconi; and Marta Mazza and Pierluigi Moriconi from the local Soprintendenza. In Ravenna, Dea Saragoni kindly allowed access to Palazzo Bacinetti. In Sigmaringen, Anette Hähnel helped with research material from the Hohenzollern-Sigmaringen archives.

Two art historians, above all, have been huge sources of inspiration during this project, and I am very grateful for the constantly enlightening conversations I have had with them: Davide Gasparotto and Nathaniel Silver. I am always stimulated by their work and cannot thank them enough.

Thank you also to Guido Beltramini, Fausto Calderai, the late Giulia Maria Crespi, Alessandro Delpriori, Mauro Magliani, Scott Nethersole, Carlo Orsi, Benedetta Possati, Monsignor Zvonimir Seršić, and Claudia and Mara Vittori.

My biggest thanks go to Michał Przygoda. I simply would not be able to do any of this without him by my side.

Xavier F. Salomon
Deputy Director and Peter Jay Sharp Chief Curator

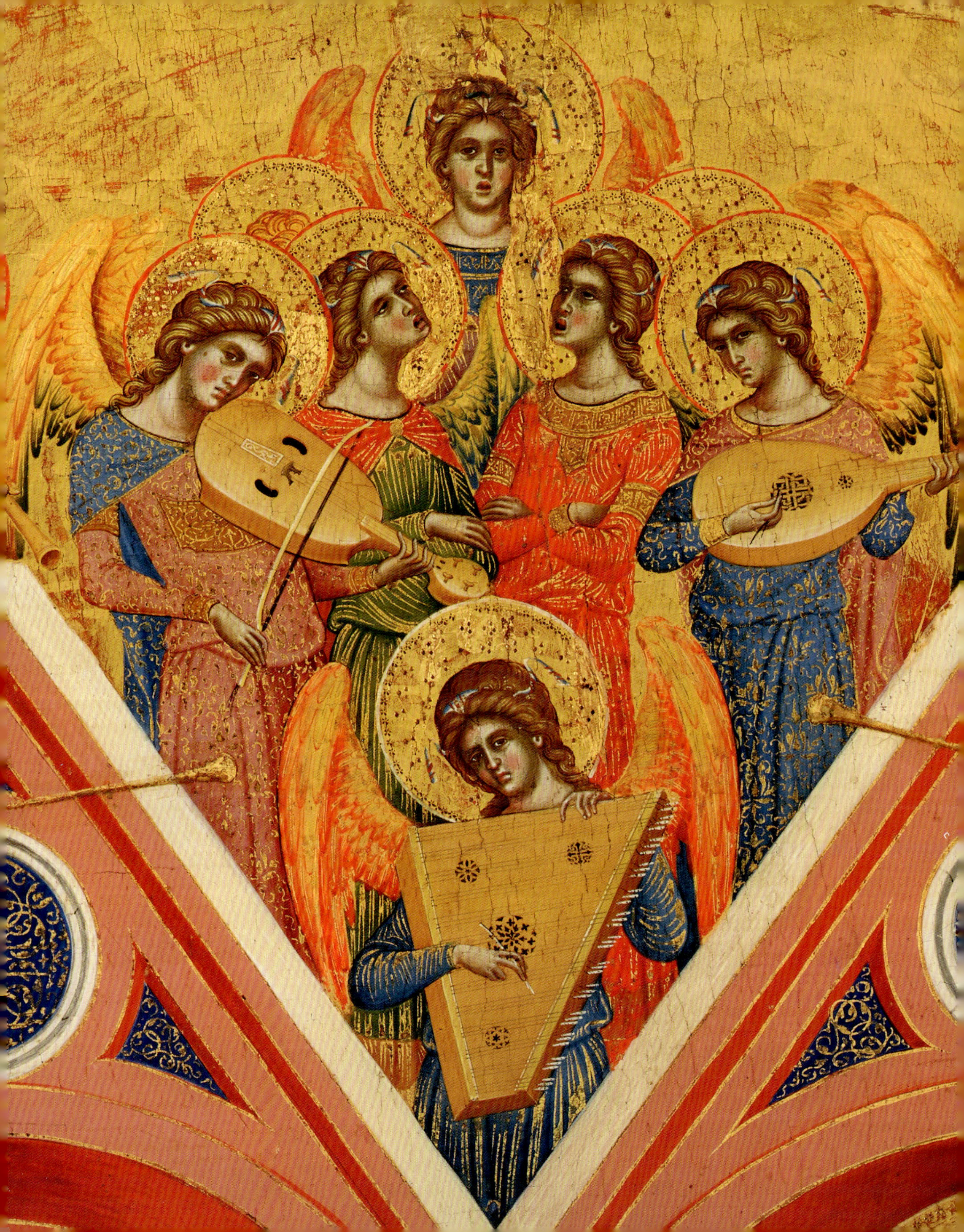

A MULTITUDE OF THE HEAVENLY HOST

Nico Muhly

Paolo Veneziano's *Coronation of the Virgin* is a panel of pure theater and music. As a tableau, there is an obvious formality to it, but much of the space is taken up with noise-making. The instrumentalists and vocalists are all playing the instruments of the fourteenth century, which is, of course, thrilling to the modern musician: it implies that the artist had seen these instruments played up-close and heard them either individually or in consort. As a composer, I am fascinated with what it must sound like in an artist's head to paint an instrument. When I write words, it is a relatively simple endeavor to hear them in my head or, indeed, speak them aloud while writing. Writing music, on the other hand, is more complicated, even though it's my job. Sometimes it's an act of transcription: I have a conception of what it's going to sound like "in reality," more or less, and then the act of notation is more like pausing a video and writing down what's happening frame by frame. The more instruments there are, the more complicated it gets; you have to keep track of the vertical aggregation of sound at the same time as all of the individual details of each instrument, which requires looking at a single moment from a satellite and then under a microscope nearly simultaneously.

Paolo has a practical musical fluency, encoded and elaborated in the preexisting imagery of the Coronation of the Virgin. He's painted many of the traditional elements of depictions of the Coronation: Mary, linked with the moon, and Jesus, linked with the sun, personified versions of which are under their feet. We see Mary's crown and halo, with its elaborate diapering and elegant position almost in the middle of the architectural elements behind her, as opposed to Jesus's, which is less formally and more realistically obscuring the structure behind him, indicating not only his relative height but a sense of the spiritual being significantly closer to the viewer. Further elongating Jesus's figure, we see his scepter, a thin, nearly vertical line of authority. Jesus and Mary are painted in a state of sumptuary luxury, the costly blue robes unique to just this pair amid the sixteen other figures.

Above them, we have the company of heaven, depicted not abstractly on clouds but more realistically in a kind of minstrels' gallery, cluttering the upper portion of the panel with a formal symmetry but with an implication of a serious racket. The first time I saw this image, I gasped audibly. I think about the book of Psalms as an orchestra and choir readying themselves for a concert. The book is littered with references to singing, making joyful noises, and, as we move through the chapters, things begin to get a bit more specific. Psalm 33 encourages us as follows: "Acknowledge ye to the Lord in an harp; sing ye to him in a psaltery of ten strings." Psalm 95 gets more theatrical, encouraging us to shout joyfully right before acknowledging that it is God's hands that have crafted the earth from its depths to its peaks—the windows are open and the song draws the eyes and the heart back to nature. Psalm 98 draws the connection closer still, describing a much louder call-and-response:

> Make a loud noise, and rejoice, and sing praise. Sing unto the Lord with the harp; with the harp and the voice of a psalm. With trumpets and sound of cornet make a joyful noise before the Lord, the King. Let the sea roar, and the fulness thereof; the world, and they that dwell therein. Let the floods clap their hands: let the hills be joyful together.

Here, whatever practical and worldly music-making we can make is answered by the whole of nature itself making noise: the seas roar, the floods clap their hands (a concept, I will confess, I've never quite grasped—perhaps waves crashing on the shore?): the delicate sound of a harp calls forth what essentially sounds like a world-shattering amount of noise and activity. The way trees sway elegantly while being violently denuded in the videos of nuclear-bomb tests in the 1950s came to mind fleetingly as I reread this verse.

Psalm 100 gets even more specific. Here, we, seen as pastured sheep, enter into God's porches, gates, courtyards: music is bringing us physically closer in a tangible way, starting with urban planning and moving into more domestic architecture. This particular psalm is known in various choral traditions as the "Jubilate" and has been set by countless composers, often in a paired setting with the significantly longer text of the Te Deum. This psalm, in agreement with No. 95, encourages us:

> Make a joyful noise unto the Lord, all ye lands. Serve the Lord with gladness: come before his presence with singing. Know ye that the Lord he is God: it is he that hath made us, and not we ourselves; we are his people, and the sheep of his pasture. Enter into his gates with thanksgiving, and into his courts with praise: be thankful unto him, and bless his name. For the Lord is good; his mercy is everlasting; and his truth endureth to all generations.

This is a much more immediate representation of how music, noise, and singing bring us into God's presence. The final psalm, No. 150, is an absolute riot of noise—obsessive, repetitive, enumerative—and it describes an orchestra:

> Praise ye the Lord. Praise God in his sanctuary: praise him in the firmament of his power. Praise him for his mighty acts: praise him according to his excellent greatness. Praise him with the sound of the trumpet: praise him with the psaltery and harp. Praise him with the timbrel and dance: praise him with stringed instruments and organs. Praise him upon the loud cymbals: praise him upon the high sounding cymbals. Let every thing that hath breath praise the Lord. Praise ye the Lord.

This is thrilling stuff: all of the implied lone musicians and small ensembles and flock-like groups of people described by the other 149 psalms are finally answered here by "every thing that hath breath" praising God. I defy you to go to a *Messiah* community sing-along and not have some form of religious tingle. I'm normally completely mortified by things like this, but it still gets me every time. (That and late-night showings of *The Wicker Man*, itself a movie about music in a variety of ways. Is it not through the local musicians that we begin to suspect something sexually inappropriate is happening at the Inn, some dark magic at work in the deconsecrated churchyard, around the maypole and in various other fertility rituals?) It is worth noting that composers have been setting to music the text of Psalm 150 forever; in terms of modern compositions, I would direct you to Steve Reich's *Tehillim* (4th movement), Stravinsky's *Symphony of Psalms* (3rd movement), and George Talbot's Anglican Chant of the same psalm. Each one has a different approach to the repetitive structure. Talbot's is limited by the way such chants are performed liturgically, which is a constantly repeated chord structure (here, conducive to the repetitive nature of the text). Reich's, in the Hebrew, is ecstatic and secretly literal, where he introduces a tuned cymbal as a nod to the scripture and to Stravinsky's *Rite of Spring*. And Stravinsky's is detached and stylized in such a way that repeated listenings unveil more and more layers of compositional brilliance in setting this text in a style somewhere between a hymn and a gallop. These composers take advantage of the way in which these texts are so pervasive, and, as nobody knows how they would have been sung at the time of their composition, there is a lack of historical tradition easily replaceable with musical brilliance. In the etymologically radical sense of the word, these composers shine different lights on the text.

Paolo has the benefit here of the story of the Coronation of the Virgin not being in the biblical text, so tradition and scripture can combine into more of a fantasia on a theme. To this end, we have the whole orchestra with us: shawms, drums, zithers, portative organs, trumpets. When I first saw this image in real life, I laughed: *imagine* the sound of all of this happening together? Even played delicately, the combination of instruments to modern ears would feel quite avant-garde, almost feral. One can imagine, of course, that Paolo had either heard this precise combination of instruments played at once, or that he'd heard smaller subdivisions in liturgical contexts. Orchestras and operas were, in his time, unknown; we begin to see things resembling operas in Italy around the end of the sixteenth century, and orchestras significantly later. Paolo's imagination is the composer and conductor here, and he is rightly celebrated for the incredibly accurate way the instruments are painted, as well as the positions in which they are played and held.

Whenever I tell non-musicians that I'm a composer, among the first questions that arises is whether or not I can play all the instruments in the orchestra. I am often embarrassed to say no but can then expand: even if I don't have the explicit technical knowledge of how a bassoon works in the sense of holding it in my hands and making it sound like a bassoon as opposed to a reed and a piece of wood with some metal details, I have a number of bassoonist friends who can talk me through these things, show me why what I've written is idiomatic or easy, and point to examples from the repertoire. Through years and years of study, I have absorbed the way that one instrument functions in context, from its sixteenth-century ancestors through Bach and Mozart and Stravinsky and onward to the present. It's about observing how the thing works and seeing it in different lights; I often claim (perhaps as an expression of shame and defensiveness) to hear an obsession with the *technical* at the expense of the *musical* when, for instance, a great violinist writes a piece of violin music: the listener can sometimes perceive a little feedback loop creating an obstacle to a larger, more zoomed-out emotional engagement.

Paolo depicts pairs of instruments, stereophonically separated around the central axis of the panel, with handheld plucked and bowed stringed instruments closest to the center and the long trumpets and drums toward the edges. Just behind Christ and Mary, we see two seraphim, each playing a portative organ. Modern organs have become giant machines—the largest instruments in the world, I would guess, disguising their origins as woodwinds. The early portative organs depicted here would be controlled by bellows, allowing the dynamics to fluctuate as needed; these instruments are the colleagues of the flutes and trumpets above but sonically linked to the human voice and a deeply intimate sense of breath. If you live somewhere within an hour of one of these instruments, do try to arrange a viewing and perhaps an experiment with it as a musical instrument and as a machine. There is something slightly ridiculous about these two seraphim (with *The Shining*-like near-identical faces) peeking around that building, with their elegant little lipsticks of slippers. Despite this, I hear great potential in the sonic possibilities of two identical organs played in stereo. If we were to hear this in some kind of literal way, the ensemble upstairs would have its sound smoothed out by the two organs on the lower axis, much as a modern organ accompanying a choir singing a hymn tends to focus the pitch and the rhythm of the more vagrant sheep in the flock.

This panel can be heard in the larger context of the images of Mary and Jesus and their sonic relationship. The Annunciation is a duet: Gabriel is tasked with finding Mary, he turns up and gives her some shocking news. He is often depicted in a sort of glute-enhancing lunge: a combination of aggression and genuflection. The birth of Jesus is itself a very noisy affair: we are invited to picture shepherds in their fields (here, representing all of us) surprised in the middle of the night by a bright light all around, and an angel standing before them. After some brief introductions by the angel:

> … suddenly there was with the angel a multitude of the heavenly host praising God, and saying: Glory to God in the highest, and on earth peace, good will toward men.

This is an absolutely terrifying sonic moment. One can't imagine that shepherds living in first-century Palestine were accustomed to loud noises or bright lights, so this occurrence would have been a life-changing sensory overload.

We then leave the supernatural realm: We can imagine Mary singing to Jesus during his infancy, and there are countless musical examples from the pre-Renaissance until the present day in which we are encouraged to think on this tender moment. Thereafter, in the canonical biblical account, the rest of his life was spent in the more standard oratorial style of a teacher, giving either a lecture to a crowd or a seminar to a select few. Even the Beatitudes, in which he outlines the blessed octave of the downtrodden to the multitudes, contain a sonic intimacy in the form of bread and wine in quotidian practice. The noises surrounding him intensify toward the end of his life: the braying of the donkey during the entrance to Jerusalem, weeping (according to Luke) at the gates of the city, and then, of course, all the goings-on in Holy Week, from crying out in the garden of Gethsemane to the Last Supper.

The hours before his death are described as highly stylized utterances. I hope nobody ever has to hear the sounds of a voice coming from a body in that much anguish, a Roman's spear wound in his side, speaking to his mother from a great and terrible height; or to his mother, long deceased, with a policeman's knee on his neck.

An earthquake ensues, as well as the rending of the veil of the temple: whatever the ripping sound of a piece of purple fabric the size of a small house might be, it was certainly not familiar to the denizens of Jerusalem at that time. We can then hear the most intimate conversation, a twin to the lullaby: whatever private words she whispers as she holds the body of her son.

What better way, then, to celebrate their next meeting than to invite the Celestial Philharmonic? The members of the band are depicted as realistically as possible, but they are not all looking at Jesus and Mary—as in many other versions of this same scene. Some of them are looking at each other, with intensity and concentration. One can imagine the zither player at the top right being distracted by the event below, and one can see the percussionist at the bottom left straining to see the lutenist's cue. They are apart from, yet part of, the space: the depiction of the trumpets' bells crossing in front of the dividing screen, the subtle ways the rightmost shawm player has moved the bell of his instrument, and the way the angel playing the drum has his elbow in front of the dividing structure all imply a permeability between foreground and background.

Even in modern times, we would consider this number of instruments to be an orchestra rather than a chamber ensemble. This noise would have been significantly louder and thicker than the usual trios and quartets we see in the art of this time, and there is something so realistic about the precision with which these instruments are being held that makes me near certain that Paolo was not using solely his imagination to paint such an orchestra; there must have been some kind of liturgical precedent and/or an act of significant musical transference in the mind of the artist. When I look at this image, I can hear exactly what the collected sound must have been like, even if I don't know what music they were playing. I would like to think that the artist, in painting it, became a kind of composer, imagining each instrument's particular exigencies and, with each addition, creating an aggregate of sound getting bigger and bigger, filling up a home, a church, a town square, a city, the countryside, the rocks, the mountains, the seas, and the rivers until *every thing that has breath* has heard it, and knows how to shout back.

Regina coeli, laetare, alleluia;
Quia quem meruisti portare, alleluia,
Resurrexit, sicut dixit, alleluia:
Ora pro nobis Deum, alleluia.

(Queen of heaven, rejoice, alleluia;
The Son you merited to bear, alleluia,
Has risen as he said, alleluia:
Pray to God for us, alleluia.)

Regina Coeli antiphon

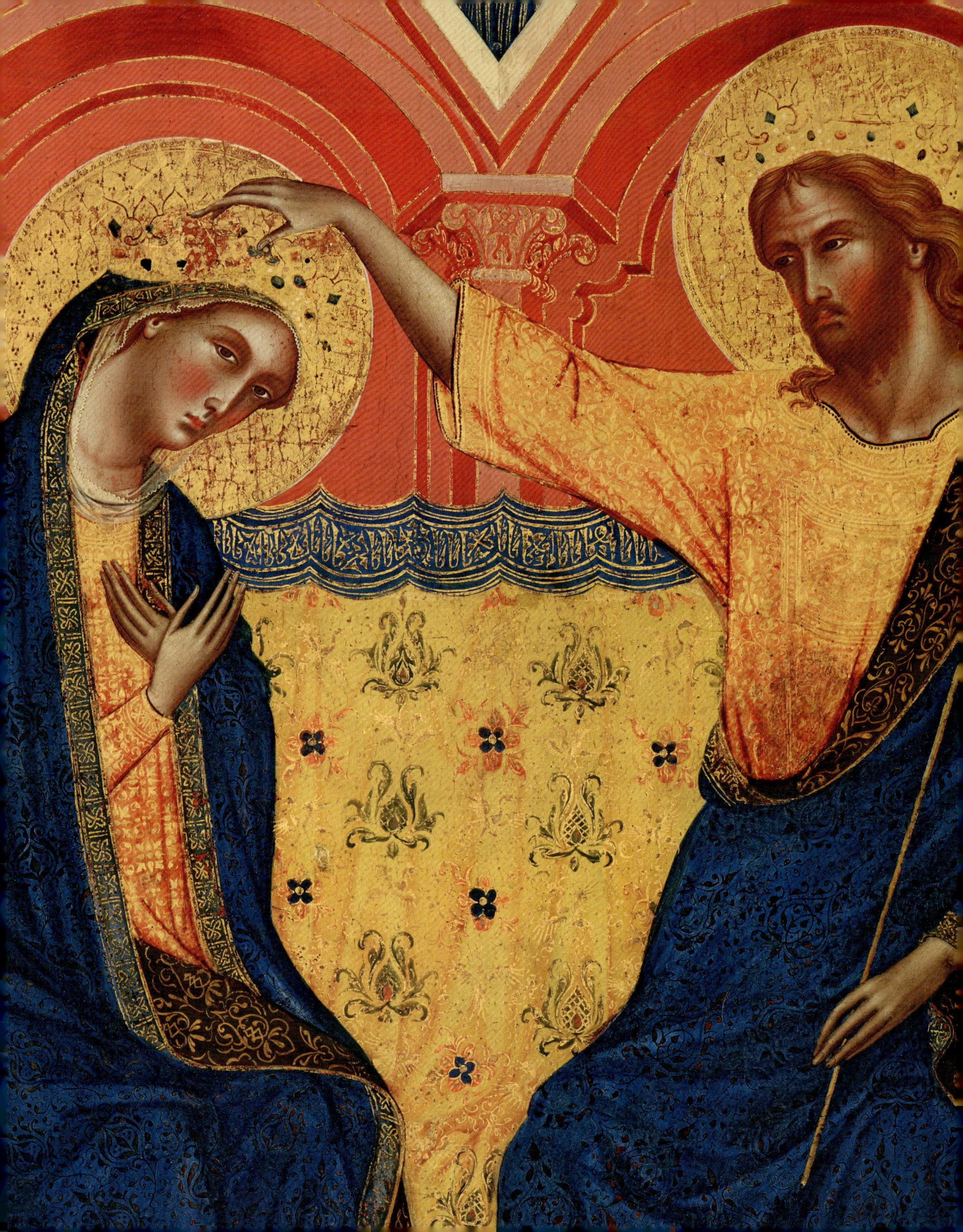

PAOLO VENEZIANO'S CORONATION OF THE VIRGIN

Xavier F. Salomon

> La parola evoca intorno all'origliere gli obliati: Lorenzo Veneziano e Simone da Cusighe e Catarino e Iacobello e Maestro Paolo e il Giambono e il Semitecolo e Antonio e Andrea e Quirizio da Murano e tutta la famiglia laboriosa per cui il colore, che doveva poi divenire emulo del fuoco, fu preparato nell'isola ardente delle fornaci.[1]
>
> —Gabriele d'Annunzio, *Il Fuoco*, 1900

Fig. 1
Paolo Veneziano with Giovanni Veneziano
Detail of *The Coronation of the Virgin*, 1358
Tempera on panel
43¼ × 27 in. (109.9 × 68.6 cm)
The Frick Collection, New York

Trecento Venice

A chronicler at the time writes that in the early morning of September 12, 1316, "almost all the inhabitants of Venice and elsewhere" assembled at the Doge's Palace, headquarters of the city's government and residence of its head of state.[2] They were there to celebrate the birth of three cubs to the two lions King Frederick III of Sicily (1272–1337) had gifted to the Venetian state. A young man named Paolo—most probably in his teens and beginning his career as a painter in Venice around that time—may very well have been among the crowd of onlookers. A few years later, in the summer of 1321, that same young man may have witnessed the brief diplomatic visit to Venice of the poet Dante Alighieri (1265–1321), who would die of malaria a few weeks later, in Ravenna. In January 1324, Paolo may also have observed the funeral and burial of Marco Polo (1254–1324), the Venetian merchant who, between the 1270s and 1292, traveled to and lived at the court of Kublai Khan (1215–1294) in China and recounted the tales of his travels while in prison in Genoa. These were the eventful times in which "Maestro Paolo"—

one of the first recorded and most influential painters in the early history of the Republic of Venice—lived and worked in Venice. In 1358, Paolo would paint *The Coronation of the Virgin* (fig. 1), his last documented work and one of the Frick's most important early Italian paintings.

Venice during Paolo's lifetime was a prosperous city of about one hundred thousand inhabitants—a mercantile state governed by an oligarchy, at the head of which stood the doge, elected by other members of the local nobility, for life.[3] The Venetian Republic still basked in the inglorious grandeur of having led the Fourth Crusade to the Sack of Constantinople, in April 1204. The episode marked the culmination of the long and complex relationship between Venice and the Byzantine Empire—dating to the legendary foundation of Venice on March 25 in the year 421—and brought success to the Italian city on the worldwide stage, while that of the imperial power waned. The history of Venice in the fourteenth century, the Trecento, is certainly to be measured against the decline of the Byzantine Empire, and the absence of the papacy from Rome, during its Avignon "captivity," between 1309 and 1376. The Trecento was for Venice a challenging time, "the hardest century, perhaps, in her history," as the historian John Julius Norwich described it.[4] It was a period of social and political upheaval and natural disaster. This was the world in which the painter Paolo grew up and worked.

During most of Paolo's life, Venice was in conflict with Genoa, the other powerful maritime Italian republic, with wars between the two states invariably ending with Genoese victories, even if mostly feeble ones. In 1298, the Genoese defeated the Venetians at Curzola (the battle in which Marco Polo was captured); another crushing defeat came at Porto Longo, in September 1354. During the intervening years, the two cities were seldom at peace. Venice, however, was not only at war with Genoa. In 1339, Venice defeated the Scaligeri of Verona and conquered inland territories on the *terraferma*, including Conegliano, Castelfranco, and Treviso. And between 1356 and 1358, the city was at war with Hungary, with the forces of King Lajos the Great of Hungary (1326–1382) ultimately conquering all of Dalmatia, which had been under the rule of the Republic of Venice.

It was a turbulent time for Venice. In 1297, the government passed what became known as the Serrata del Maggior Consiglio (the Great Council Lockout), making participation in the Great Council of the state hereditary, open to only a relatively small number of aristocratic families. This firmly established Venice as a republican oligarchy, a crucial feature of the Republic's political character until its demise at the end of the eighteenth century. In the 1300s, Venice suffered three major conspiracies against its government. The first, in 1300, was organized by Marin Bocconio—and was motivated in part by dissatisfaction with the Serrata—and concluded with the hanging of Bocconio and his fellow conspirators in the Piazzetta di San Marco.[5] In 1310, on June 15, the feast day of San Vito, Bajamonte Tiepolo (d. 1328), together with members of two other aristocratic families—the Querini and Badoer—attempted to overthrow Doge Pietro Gradenigo (1251–1311).[6] It was a thunderous night, and the bad weather, together with the disorganization of the plotters and the lack of support from the populace, doomed the endeavor. The hero of the day was Giustina Rossi, an old woman living on the Merceria, who threw a stone mortar from the window at Tiepolo when the conspirators entered Piazza San Marco but missed and hit and killed his standard bearer, causing the leader of the revolt to retreat. Tiepolo was subsequently condemned to exile by the state. The third conspiracy, in April 1355, was led by the doge himself, Marino Faliero (1274–1355), who plotted to defeat the aristocracy of Venice and make himself prince of Venice.[7] The plot was discovered, the conspirators hanged from the windows of the Doge's Palace, and Faliero was "beheaded for his crimes" (DECAPITATI PRO CRIMINIBUS) on the staircase of the palace. The conspiracies of Bajamonte Tiepolo and Marino Faliero would endure in the collective memory of Venice for centuries to come (fig. 2).

The Trecento was also a time of divine and natural reckoning for Venice. Because of a disagreement over the sovereignty of Ferrara, Venice came into direct conflict with the papacy (not an unusual occurrence for Venice) and as a result was under papal interdict—all of its citizens effectively excommunicated—from 1309 to 1313. In February 1340, major flooding devastated the city. And with the spring of 1348 came the arrival in Venice of the Black Death, which would ravage the city. At the plague's peak, approximately six hundred people died every day, and by the end of it, more than half the population had perished. The horror of the epidemic on the Italian peninsula can be grasped from these poignant words of the contemporary Sienese chronicler Agnolo di Tura: "No one wept for the dead, because everyone expected death himself."[8]

There were of course some positive events during Master Paolo's lifetime, among them, improvements to the urban fabric of Venice. In the fourteenth century, following the paving of Piazza San Marco at the end of

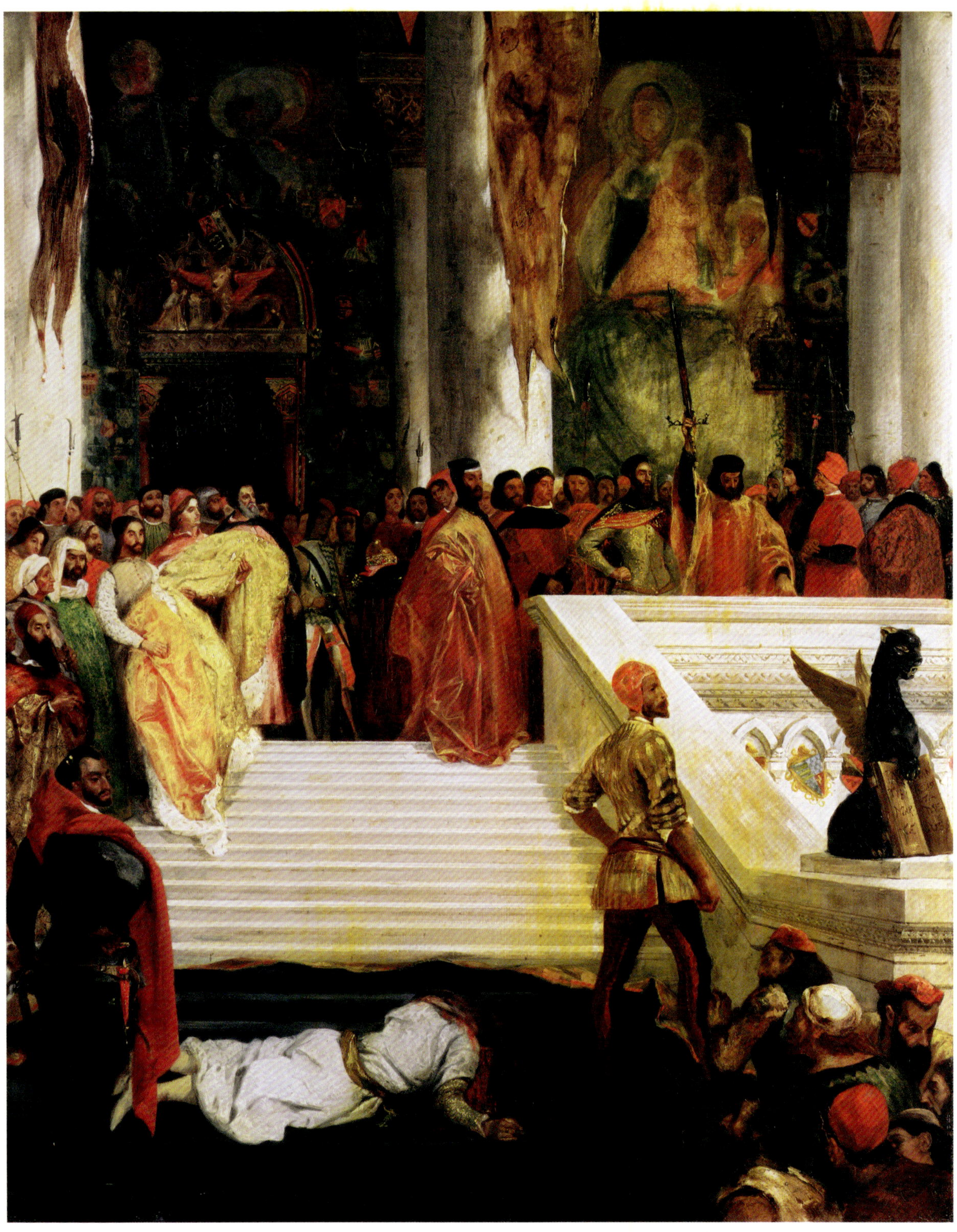

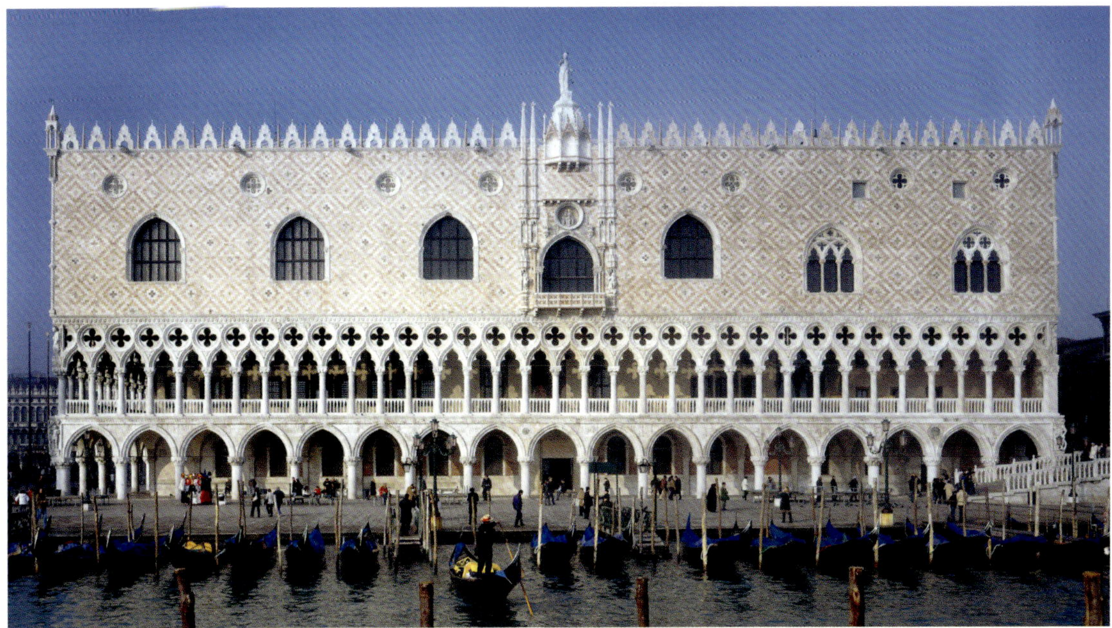

the thirteenth century, most of Venice's *campi* (squares) and *calli* (streets) were paved in stone for the first time. Many of the wells of the city were created, and the Arsenal—the main shipyards of Venice—was substantially enlarged. Two enormous churches of the mendicant orders were also under construction. Santi Giovanni e Paolo (or San Zanipolo in Venetian dialect)—the Dominican church in the northern part of the city—was completed in 1333, at which point construction to enlarge it immediately got underway. The main Franciscan church—Santa Maria Gloriosa dei Frari—on the opposite side of Venice, was completed in October 1338, and reconstruction of it too began immediately and continued through most of the fourteenth century. In January 1341, work began on a new Doge's Palace, under the architect Pietro Baseggio (d. 1354). By 1365, the entire south facade and most of the west one—as we know them today—were built (fig. 3). Work on the palace was to continue for the next eighty years, finished only in 1425. The architectural and artistic history of Venice intersected with some of its historic events. Filippo Calendario (1315–1355)—one of the earliest architects of the Doge's Palace—was one of the men condemned to death for high treason for his part in the Marino Faliero coup. He was among those hanged from the windows of the palace he was building.

Fig. 2
Eugène Delacroix
The Execution of the Doge Marino Faliero, 1825–26
Oil on canvas
57⅝16 × 44¹³⁄16 in.
(145.6 × 113.8 cm)
The Wallace Collection, London

Fig. 3. Doge's Palace, Venice

Fig. 4
Monument to Doge Andrea Dandolo, after 1354
Marble
Baptistery, Basilica of St. Mark's, Venice

An important period in Paolo's life was during the reign of Doge Andrea Dandolo (r. 1343–54), who was not only a scholar who compiled one of the most comprehensive histories of Venice but also Paolo's most important patron.[9] Dandolo was buried in a grandiose monument in the baptistery of St. Mark's—the last doge to be buried inside the basilica (fig. 4). The final years of Paolo's life were most likely under Doge Lorenzo Celsi (r. 1361–65). By then the most prominent painter in Venice, Paolo may have witnessed the celebrations in September 1361 that welcomed Duke Rudolf IV of Austria (1339–1365) to Venice. He had most likely died by the time Peter I of Lusignan, king of Cyprus (1328–1369), came to Venice a year later, in the fall of 1362, and when the poet Petrarch (1304–1374) moved to the city, also in late 1362.[10]

In his groundbreaking 1951 book *Painting in Florence and Siena after the Black Death: The Arts, Religion, and Society in the Mid-Fourteenth Century*, the American art historian Millard Meiss examined artistic production in the two Tuscan cities between 1350 and 1375.[11] Discussing the economic and social history of Tuscany, he focused on the period after the Black Death in the summer of 1348. As in Venice, more than half of the populations of Florence and Siena had been decimated by the plague. Among the victims were prominent painters such as Bernardo Daddi (ca. 1280–1348) and Pietro (ca. 1280–1348) and Ambrogio (ca. 1290–1348) Lorenzetti. Meiss discussed how artists such as Andrea di Cione "Orcagna" (ca. 1308–1368), his brother Nardo di Cione (d. 1366), Andrea da Firenze (1319–1379), Giovanni da Milano (ca. 1325–ca. 1370), Luca di Tommè (ca. 1330–1389), Bartolo di Fredi (ca. 1330–1410), and the elusive (and possibly non-existent) Barna da Siena compare with their colleagues of the previous generation, like Bernardo Daddi, Taddeo Gaddi (1290–1366), and the Lorenzetti brothers. He wrote that "the painting of the third quarter of the century, more religious in a traditional sense, more ecclesiastical, and more akin to the art of an earlier time, may reflect these profound social changes in Florence and Siena, or rather the taste and the quality of piety that they brought into prominence."[12] In the same way, the life and work of Paolo can only be fully understood in the context of the times in which he lived: the feverish building campaigns of the Doge's Palace and the mendicant churches, the papal interdict, the floods and the plague, the wars and conspiracies—the rich tapestry of Trecento Venice.

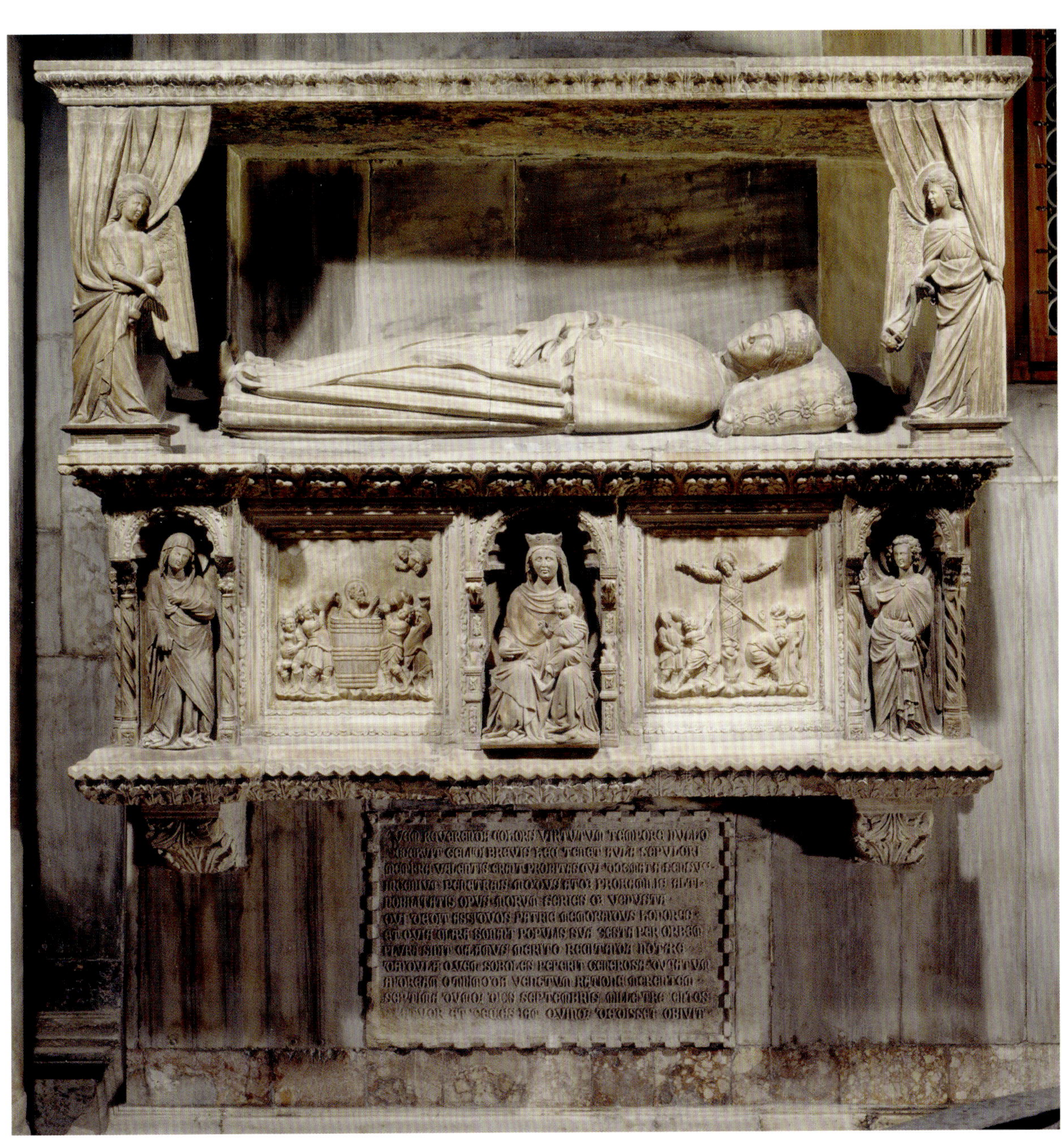

Paulus de Veneciis

In 1333, the painter Paolo from Venice (PAVLVS DE VENECIIS) signed a painting that depicted the Dormition of the Virgin, the central panel of a large polyptych probably painted for the high altar of the Franciscan church of San Lorenzo in Vicenza.[13] The panel is flanked by images of St. Francis of Assisi and St. Anthony of Padua (fig. 5)—both standing—which places the polyptych firmly within the circles of a Franciscan commission for San Lorenzo. The surviving three panels show only part of the overall work, but the polyptych must have originally included other standing saints, possibly a predella, and half-length representations of other saints on the upper level. With statuesque figures of the Franciscan saints, a Dormition scene deeply embedded in Byzantine prototypes but colored by emotions, the tender expression on the face of Christ as he holds the representation of the soul of his mother and looks at her dead body, and the crying figures of the apostles around the bier of the Virgin, the polyptych must have been quite impressive. The painting denotes a taste for prized materials such as gold and textiles, and elegant effects, like the rhythm of the heads of the angelic hierarchies witnessing the death and assumption of the Virgin and their extended wings framing the scene at the top, showing Christ carrying his mother's soul to heaven. The San Lorenzo Polyptych introduces into history "the first master known to us, almost the founder—as Paolo has been called—of the Venetian school of painting."[14] Paolo emerges on the scene as a fully formed artist.[15] In the same year, he signed and dated another work—a *Death of St. Francis of Assisi*—which was described in 1650 as being in the collection of Count Girolamo Gualdo in Vicenza but is now lost. It may have been the central compartment of another polyptych for the same church of San Lorenzo.[16]

The prehistory of Paolo from Venice—now commonly known as Paolo Veneziano—is shrouded in mystery. Not a single work by him is dated or documented before 1333, and scholars have long debated his birth date, as well as which works he may (or may not) have painted before 1333.[17] Some information on his family background can, however, be gleaned from two documents from the second half of the 1330s. One was written in 1335 by Oliviero Forzetta (ca. 1300–1373), a notary from Treviso who was also a cloth merchant, moneylender, collector, and bibliophile. Forzetta was closing up his house in Venice and moving back to Treviso, and, for the purposes of the move, he wrote a series of notes to himself regarding business matters that required

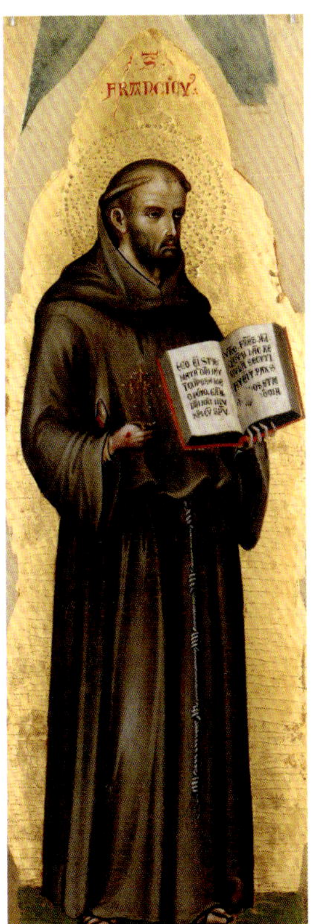

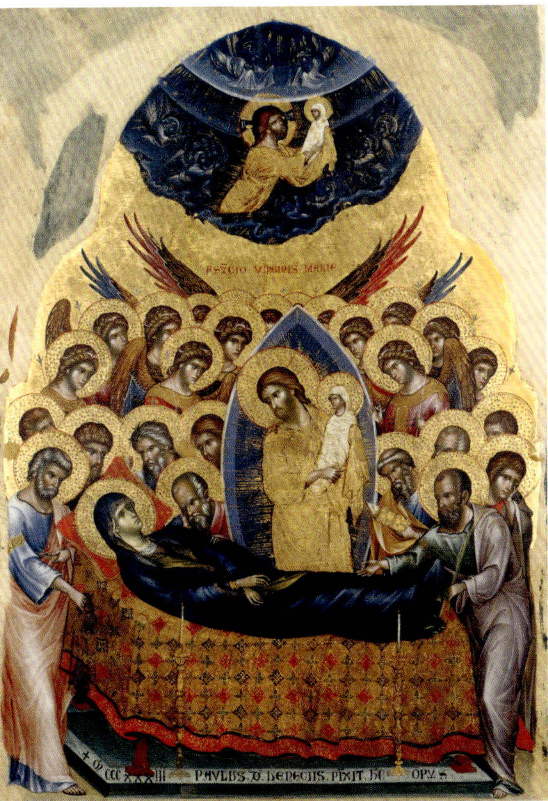

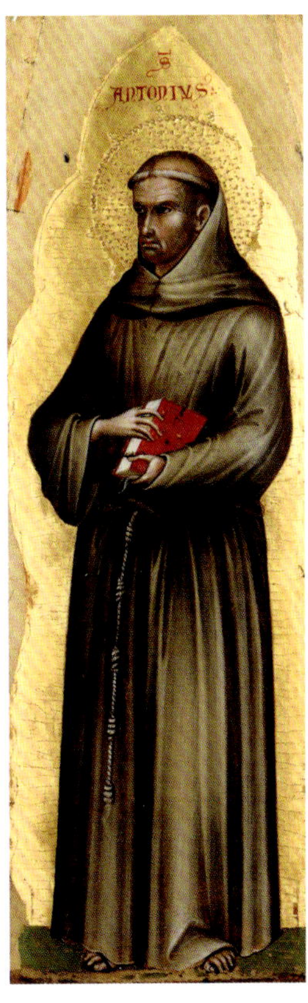

Fig. 5
Paolo Veneziano
San Lorenzo Polyptych, 1333
Tempera on panel
Left: *St. Francis of Assisi*, 35⅛ × 9⅛ in. (89 × 23 cm)
Center: *The Dormition of the Virgin*, 30¼ × 44⅛ in. (77 × 112 cm)
Right: *St. Anthony of Padua*, 35½ × 9⅛ in. (90 × 23 cm)
Musei Civici, Vicenza

his attention. These notes provide information as to his cultural and artistic interests.[18] Two goldsmiths—Giovanni Teutonico and Master Ognibene—needed to be paid for some cameos and statuettes, and a Master Francesco had to be compensated for a griffin he had painted on Forzetta's coat of arms. Forzetta also had to pay for volumes of Seneca, Ovid, Sallust, Livy, Valerius Maximus, Thomas Aquinas, and Averroes, among others he had acquired for his library. He noted that he had to collect "all the drawings" that belonged to the deceased "poor Perenzolo, son of Master Angelo" and a notebook in which Perenzolo had drawn some beautiful animals, all of which had been pawned and were now with "Masters Francesco and Stefano" at San Giovanni Nuovo. Forzetta reminds himself in his notes about a certain Master Marco, a painter who lived near the Frari in Venice.[19] For the Franciscans in Treviso, Marco had produced some "German cloths" (PANNOS THEUTONICOS)—probably some paintings on cloth (unclear if they were German in typology or style, or both). Apparently, a German friar had previously produced similar works in

Venice, and Marco had copied them and sent them to Treviso. He had also produced similar cloths and stained-glass windows for the Frari in Venice. Finally, Forzetta records that Master Marco has a brother, named Paolo—also a painter—who lives near the Frari. Paolo had made two drawings, showing the Death of St. Francis and the Dormition of the Virgin, that were similar to Marco's "German cloths" in San Francesco in Treviso. Forzetta's notes confirm that Paolo had a brother (unclear if older or younger), Marco, who was also a painter and that they both lived near the Frari and worked for the Franciscan order. Interestingly enough, writing in 1335, Forzetta mentions two drawings by Paolo with the same subject matter as that of the works he had signed in 1333 in Vicenza. Clearly, Marco and Paolo—likely in a joint workshop—produced a range of artworks for the Franciscan order: paintings, drawings, "German cloths," and stained-glass windows. Four years later, on February 25, 1339, another document records that "Master Paolo the painter, son of the late Martino the painter" sold some land in the area of Santa Maria Maggiore in Treviso, which was part of the dowry of his wife, Caterina Baldoino.[20] By this date, Paolo was resident in the *sestiere* of San Marco in Venice, near the parish of San Luca. The 1335 and 1339 documents give us a sense of Paolo's background. Both his father, Martino (d. by 1339), and his brother Marco were painters; it is therefore possible that Paolo's training took place in his father's workshop. Unfortunately, both Martino and Marco are known only through these documents, and no works can be definitively attributed to them.[21] Marco is never mentioned again, so he may also have died in the 1330s. By 1335, Paolo and Marco's workshop was near the Frari, but by 1339 Paolo alone had moved to San Luca, possibly after Marco's death. By 1339, Paolo was married, and his sons with Caterina were probably born in the early 1330s, if not earlier. Paolo, his father, and his brother were not only painters but seem to have provided designs for other types of artworks.

The 1330s saw Paolo producing both large altarpieces and smaller devotional works, still within the Franciscan circles. Two *altaroli* (portable triptychs)—one now divided among the Worcester Art Museum, the J. Paul Getty Museum in Los Angeles, and the National Gallery of Art in Washington and the other, of lower quality and likely a workshop production, now in the Galleria Nazionale in Parma—probably date to the 1330s and were painted for devotional purposes on behalf of patrons close to the Franciscan order.[22] Paolo's most complete polyptych (albeit still with some parts missing) is

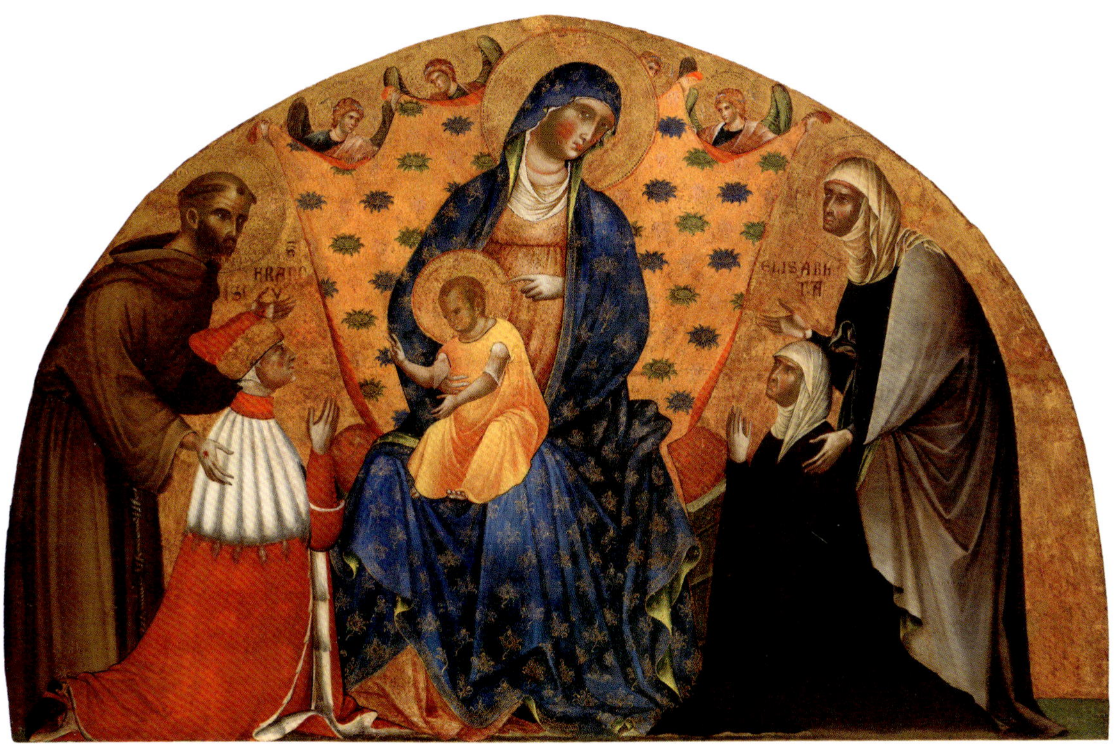

likely to have been painted in the second half of the 1330s for a Franciscan institution, the convent of Santa Chiara in Venice (fig. 6).[23] The polyptych has a central panel, depicting the Coronation of the Virgin, flanked by eight scenes, on two tiers, of the life of Christ—from the Nativity to the Ascension. Above it are six smaller scenes, four of them from the lives of saints Francis and Claire, flanked by the Pentecost and the Last Judgment. In between are slender images of the four evangelists and the prophets Isaiah and David. The cimasa, or central element at the top of the polyptych, is missing, as is a possible predella. The polyptych—with its unusual format and still, partly, in its original frame—pushes the sophistication and wealth of details of the 1333 *Dormition of the Virgin* to new heights with beautiful coloristic and formal passages and gives a good idea of how splendid the Vicenza polyptychs must have been. The polyptych was likely created during the end of the reign of Doge Francesco Dandolo, who was at the head of the Venetian state for a decade, from 1329 to 1339. After he died, on October 31, 1339, Paolo painted the lunette over his tomb in the chapter house of the Frari (fig. 7).[24]

Fig. 6 (overleaf)
Paolo Veneziano
Santa Chiara Polyptych, ca. 1335
Tempera on panel
50¼ × 112⅝ in. (128 × 286 cm)
Gallerie dell'Accademia, Venice

Fig. 7
Paolo Veneziano
Virgin and Child with Saints Francis and Elizabeth of Hungary, Presenting Doge Francesco Dandolo and His Wife Elisabetta Contarini, ca. 1339
Tempera on panel
57⅛ × 87⅞ in. (145 × 233 cm)
Santa Maria Gloriosa dei Frari, Venice

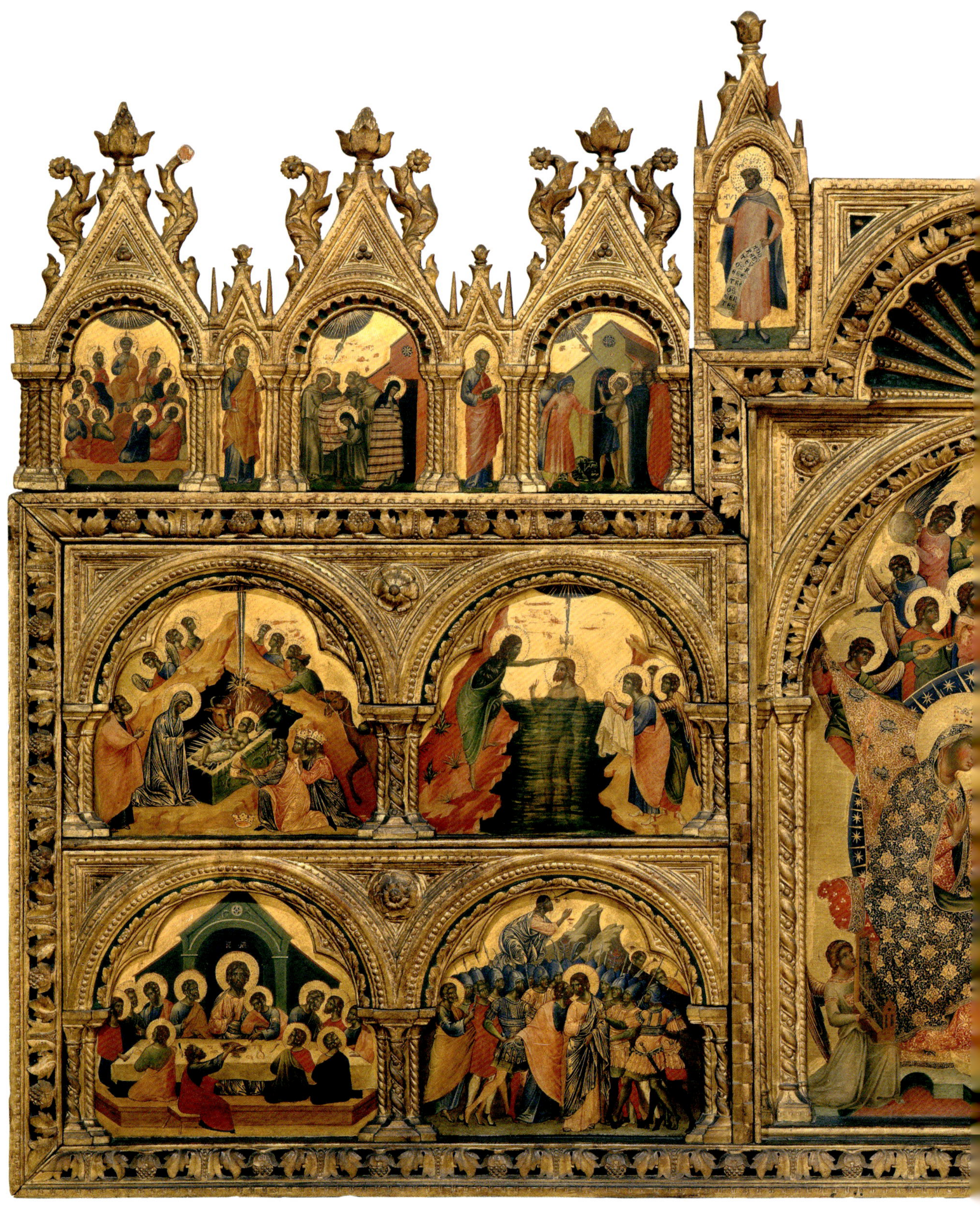

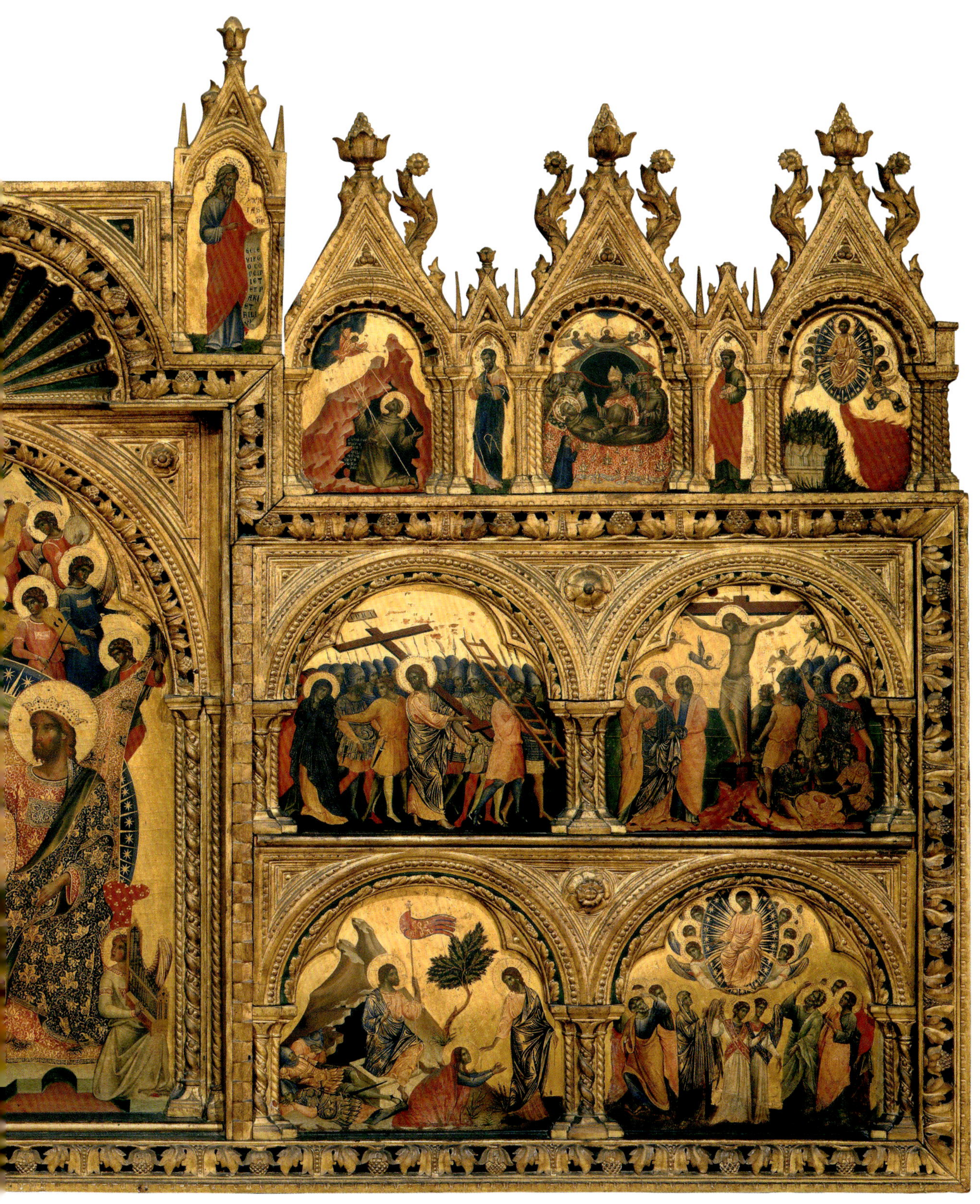

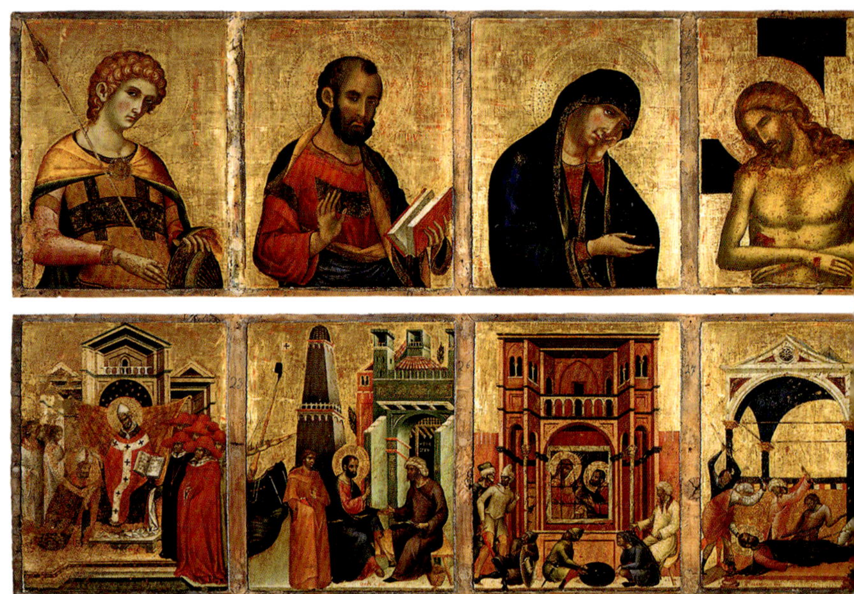

While still created in a Franciscan context—like all the previous works by Paolo known or documented today—the panel showing the dead doge and his wife Elisabetta Contarini being presented to the Virgin and Child by their respective patron saints, Francis of Assisi and Elizabeth of Hungary, is an important commission for Paolo's career. We do not know if the painting was ordered by the doge's widow and family or by the Franciscans, in whose church the doge asked to be buried; either way, the lunette of Doge Dandolo is the first instance of Paolo working at the highest level of Venetian society, creating a memorial for the deceased head of state. Even more important commissions were to follow in the next decade.

Paolo probably signed his next painting, the *Virgin and Child* (dated August 1340)—now in the Crespi collection in Milan—in the same year that he was working on the Dandolo lunette.[25] The *Virgin and Child* is likely the central panel of another large polyptych, the other parts of which are lost. From a notarized document Paolo signed as a witness on March 30, 1341, we know that he was still living in the parish of San Luca.[26] In the autumn of the following year, on September 16, 1342, "Ser Paulus pictor" was given a salary to provide decorations for a Venetian festivity, the Festa delle Marie.[27] This payment has been seen, by Michelangelo Muraro especially, as the first time in which Paolo Veneziano appears as the "official painter" of the Venetian

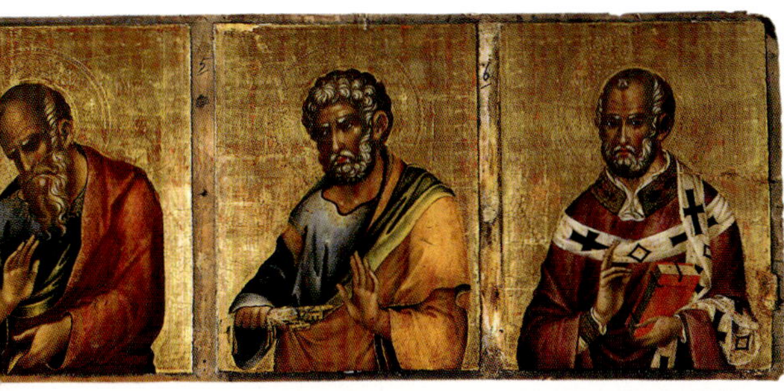

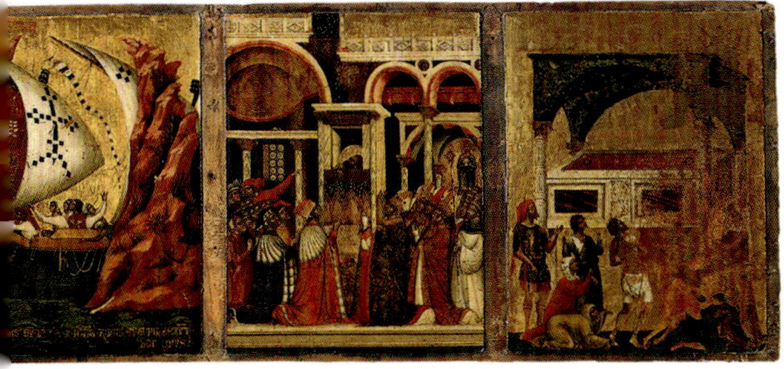

Fig. 8
Paolo, Luca, and Giovanni Veneziano
Pala Feriale, 1345
Tempera on panel, each panel
23¼ × 127¹⁵⁄₁₆ in. (59 × 325 cm)
Museo di San Marco, Venice

Republic: "The commissions for the dogal tombs and for public festivities, the presence of the artist in the Doge's Palace and in the Basilica of San Marco, establish, in my view, the fundamental stages of the line of development of Master Paolo's art."[28] This role coincided with major cultural developments in Venice, under Doge Andrea Dandolo, a distant cousin of Francesco Dandolo.[29] Paolo and his workshop were at the center of the most important art commissions in the two locations at the heart of the religious and civic life of Venice. In May 1343, the doge provided funds for the restoration of the so-called Pala d'Oro, the twelfth-century gold-and-enamel high altar of the doge's official chapel, St. Mark's.[30] On April 22, 1345, Paolo signed the painted cover designed to protect the lavish Pala d'Oro during ordinary days. Known as the Pala Feriale (weekday altarpiece), this substantial work is structured over two tiers: an upper one with half-length figures—the dead Christ at center, flanked on the left by saints George and Mark and the Virgin, and on the right by saints John the Evangelist, Peter, and Nicholas—and a lower one with seven episodes of the life, death, and miracles of St. Mark (fig. 8).[31] Set in the most prominent location in Venice, directly above the tomb of St. Mark, the patron of the state, the painting was dated by Paolo and signed by him and his two sons, Luca and Giovanni.[32] This is the first time that Paolo's children are documented. For them to be able to participate in

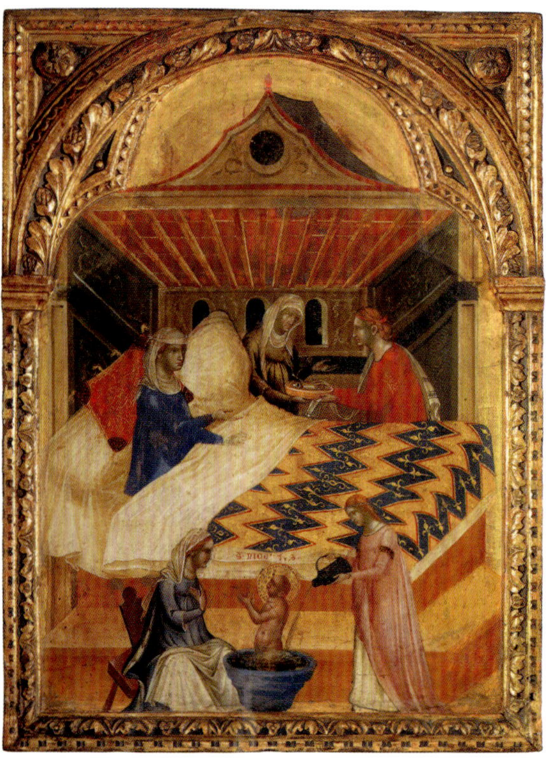

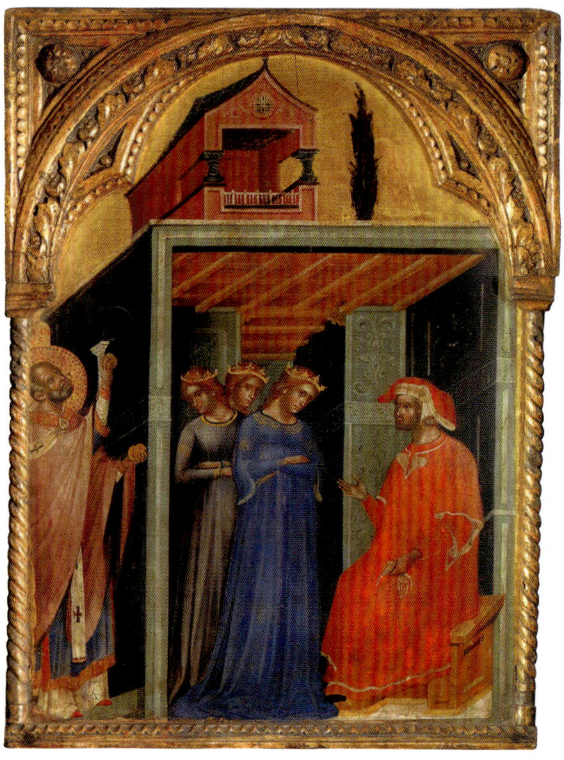

Fig. 9
Paolo Veneziano
The Birth and First Miracle of St. Nicholas, ca. 1347
Tempera on panel
29⅜ × 21½ in. (74.5 × 54.5 cm)
Contini Bonacossi Bequest, Gallerie degli Uffizi, Florence

Fig. 10
Paolo Veneziano
The Generosity of St. Nicholas, ca. 1347
Tempera on panel
29½ × 20⅞ in. (75 × 53 cm)
Contini Bonacossi Bequest, Gallerie degli Uffizi, Florence

their father's workshop, they must have been at least in their teens, born in the second half of the 1320s or around 1330 at the latest. Two other sons, Marco and Gregorio, are later documented as painters.[33] Less than two years later, on January 20, 1347, Master Paolo—still living in San Luca—was paid 20 gold ducats to paint an altarpiece for the chapel of St. Nicholas in the Doge's Palace.[34] The subject of the altarpiece is nowhere described, but two fragments with scenes from the life of St. Nicholas (figs. 9, 10) may have originally been part of this polyptych.[35] In the mid-1340s, Paolo showed a growing gift for narrative. Both the stories of St. Mark in the Pala Feriale and the two of St. Nicholas show how, while still working in a Byzantine idiom, the painter was developing a graceful manner of telling stories visually. By this point in his career, he was also the head of a thriving family workshop, with his children closely collaborating with him, according to Venetian custom.

Another *Virgin and Child*, from the parish church of Carpineta, near Cesena, was signed and dated by Paolo in 1347.[36] Roberto Longhi, in 1946, commented on the "ornamental teeming" of its decoration, especially over the surface of its depictions of textiles.[37] This panel was most likely the central compartment of a now dismembered polyptych made for an unknown location. As is evident from the first documented works, in Vicenza, Paolo was clearly producing both large altarpieces and smaller devotional works for a market that ranged from the Veneto to the western coast of the Adriatic Sea. On March 3, 1348, a man named Simun Rastić, from Ragusa (modern-day Dubrovnik) in Dalmatia, left 80 *iperperi* for a crucifix to be placed over the high altar of the Dominican church of the city; he also requested an altarpiece for the same church showing a Maestà.[38] Rastić does not mention Paolo as the author of the works, but the monumental cross (fig. 11), which remains in the church of San Domenico in Dubrovnik, is by Paolo and is most likely the one paid for by Rastić.[39] No sign remains of the Maestà or another large crucifix by Paolo later documented in the Franciscan church of Dubrovnik.[40] On April 18, 1352, Nicola Lucarić—another citizen of Ragusa—paid the

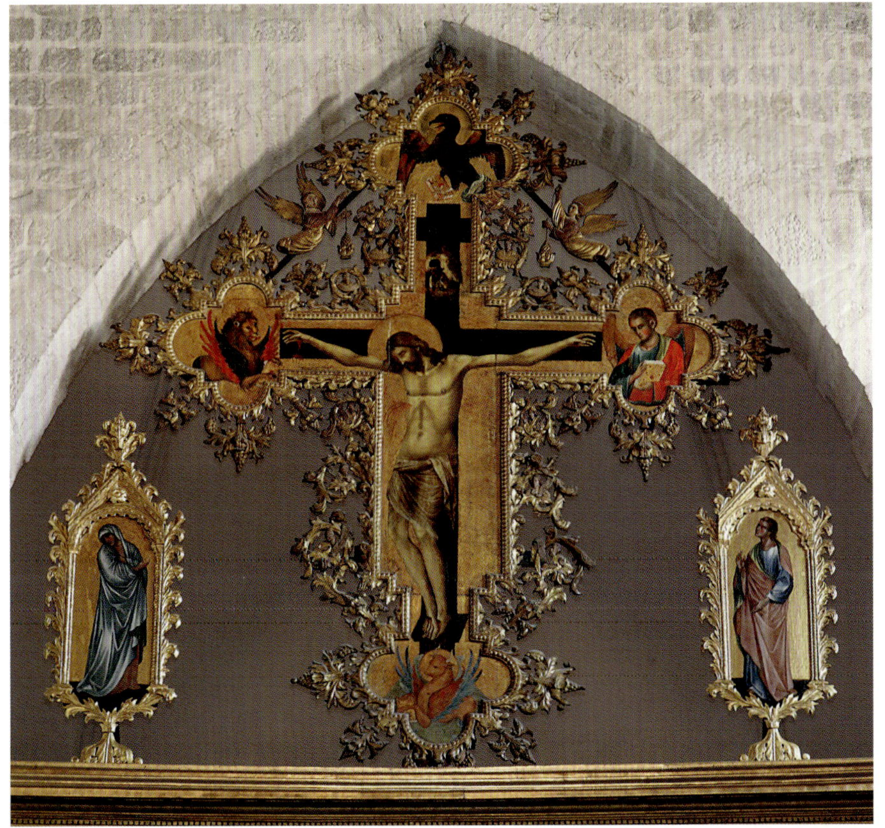

Fig. 11
Paolo Veneziano
Crucifix, 1348
Tempera on panel
162¼ × 125¼ in. (412 × 318 cm)
San Domenico, Dubrovnik

substantial sum of 150 *iperperi* to commission a polyptych by "Master Paolo Venetian painter" (Magistro Polo pintori Veneti) for the same Dominican church in Ragusa.[41] This altarpiece does not survive, but, judging from the cost, it must have been remarkable. Paolo's seemingly working mainly for a Dalmatian audience between 1348 and 1352 may be related to the Black Death in Venice. With the plague having decimated the city's population, it is likely that he focused on foreign commissions. It is also conceivable that he spent some of this time in Dalmatia, trying to avoid the plague in Venice.[42]

The Black Death of 1348 certainly had an effect on Paolo's career. All his known works of the last decade of his documented life—most of them altarpieces—were produced for locations outside of Venice, primarily along the Adriatic. Michelangelo Muraro suggested that the plague had a negative influence on Paolo's style, with the artist retreating to a more traditional, Byzantine style after the devastating effects of the epidemic.[43] Of Paolo's work after 1348, Muraro wrote, "A hieratic and superstitious immobility has definitely replaced the preciousness of colors and the luminous grace that the artist had always loved. Schemes and forms stiffen: decorations become large and opaque; profiles are reduced to larvae; the painterly technique is always hastier and more neglected."[44] No other signed works by Paolo survive from the decade after the Cesena *Virgin and Child*, but a number of dated altarpieces, all of which have stylistic similarities, have been attributed to him and his workshop. Rather than subscribing to Muraro's somewhat one-dimensional explanation of Paolo's shifting style in the 1350s, a number of factors should be considered. After undertaking prestigious commissions under Doge Andrea Dandolo, Paolo focused mostly on commissions for religious institutions outside of Venice in the last decade of his production. Many of these works were created for territories along the Adriatic Sea, under the tutelage of the Venetian Republic—the so-called *stato da mar* (dominions of the sea)—especially in Dalmatia.[45] These altarpieces, crucifixes, and devotional works were often produced in almost serial fashion and with the help of a large, well-organized workshop that included Paolo's children and other assistants.[46] Within the broader landscape of Venetian production, Paolo's altarpieces and paintings became precious commodities for an international audience.[47]

Three dated altarpieces have been attributed to Paolo and his workshop (though none of them are signed) for the period between the end of the 1340s and the mid-1350s. In 1349, the workshop dated a polyptych of the Virgin

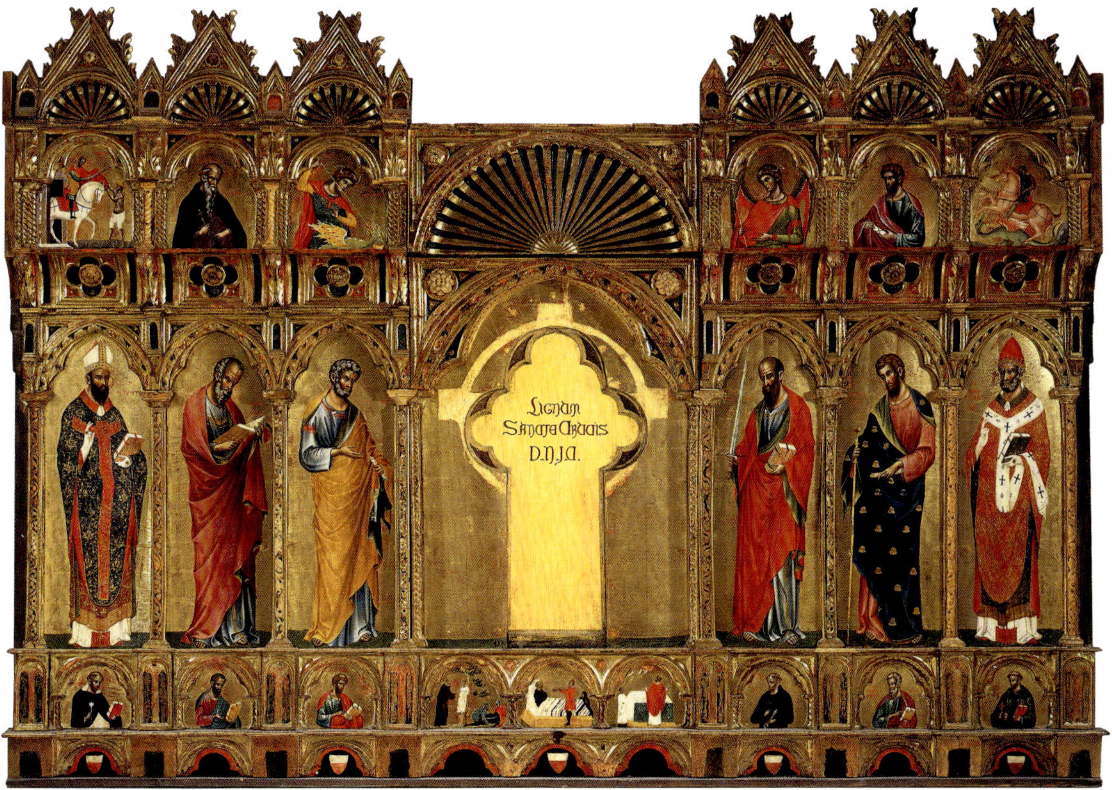

Fig. 12
Paolo Veneziano
San Giacomo Maggiore Polyptych, ca. 1350s
Tempera on panel
56 × 111 in. (142 × 281 cm)
San Giacomo Maggiore, Bologna

and Child, flanked by saints Peter, John the Baptist, John the Evangelist, and Paul, which was most recently in the church of San Martino in Chioggia, just outside Venice.[48] In 1354, another large polyptych—also with the Virgin and Child and saints Francis of Assisi, John the Baptist, John the Evangelist, and Anthony of Padua (now at the Louvre)—was painted for an unknown Franciscan institution.[49] And in April 1355, the workshop dated another polyptych, from the church of San Giorgio in Piran, with the Virgin and Child at its center, flanked by eight saints: Mary Magdalene, Nicholas of Bari, Mark, John the Baptist, John the Evangelist, Blaise, Anthony Abbot, and Catherine.[50]

The most impressive of the altarpieces from this period, however, dated on stylistic grounds to the 1350s, was for the church of San Giacomo Maggiore in Bologna (fig. 12).[51] Most likely painted for the church's chapel of the Holy Cross and designed to have a central compartment (now altered) to contain a relic of the cross, this monumental polyptych is structured on at least three levels. The relic would have been flanked by six figures of standing saints: Augustine,

John the Evangelist, and Peter on the left; and Paul, James, and Gregory the Great on the right. Above them are six smaller panels. The two at the extremities show narratives of St. Martin sharing his cloak (on the left) and St. George killing the dragon (on the right), and the other four represent half-length images of saints and archangels: Anthony Abbot, Michael, Raphael, and Luke. The lowest level—the predella—also depicts a combination of narratives and figures of saints. Three central scenes from the life of St. Nicholas of Tolentino are flanked by smaller half-length images of saints Dominic, Mark, and Luke (on the left) and Leonard, Matthew, and Francis of Assisi (on the right). The polyptych is likely missing its upper central element—its cimasa—possibly a Crucifixion. Though somewhat incomplete, the Bologna polyptych, like the Santa Chiara one from more than a decade before, demonstrates how imposing the polyptychs produced in Paolo's workshop were and why they were in such demand along the Adriatic Sea.

In September 1362, Paolo's son Marco was fined for brawling with a fisherman, and in the document for the violation he is referred to as the "son of the deceased Master Paolo the painter" (QUONDAM MAGISTRI PAULI PICTORIS).[52] So while we do not know the date of Paolo's death, we do know that by September 1362 he was no longer alive. His children and pupils, however, continued to be active after he died. Marco is documented as a painter in the 1370s and up to the 1390s.[53] We know that another son—Gregorio (GREGORIO PAULI DE VENETIIS PICTOR)—was active in Bologna in 1359, because, together with the painter Vitale da Bologna (ca. 1309–1360), he served as a witness to the signing of a surviving document.[54] In September 1366, a certain Nicholas from Zadar (who had been granted citizenship in Venice) was described as a painter who had studied for five years in Paolo's workshop.[55]

The Frick's *Coronation of the Virgin*

The last signed work by Paolo Veneziano is *The Coronation of the Virgin*, dated 1358.[56] In gold letters, over the green ground, the panel is inscribed M.C.C.C.L.V.I.I.I. / PAVLVS CVM / IOHANINVS EIV[S] / FILIV[S] / PI[N]SERV[N]T HOC OP (1358. Paolo with his son Giovannino painted this work). Having already signed the Pala Feriale, with his sons Luca and Giovanni, Paolo signed his last work with Giovanni alone, using the diminutive Giovannino. It is likely that Luca had died by then; there is no evidence of him as an artist beyond the inscription on the Pala Feriale. Giovanni, however, appears in the signatures of two works: the Pala Feriale and the Frick's *Coronation*. He may have died around the time of his father or abandoned his career as a painter soon after. A second inscription on the panel, along the base of the throne—over a blue ground and also in gold letters—recites the antiphon Regina Coeli (Queen of Heaven) dedicated to the Virgin Mary: REGINA. CELLI. LETARE / ALE / LVIA. QVEN. MERVISTI. CRIS / TVM / PORTARE. ALELVIA (Queen of Heaven, rejoice, hallelujah. You merited to bear Christ, hallelujah). A large throne occupies most of the picture plane of the panel. Painted in pink—possibly to evoke Verona marble—and decorated with gold and blue lapis lazuli, the extraordinary structure is further embellished with a yellow Cloth of Honor, decorated with motifs typical of Tartar prototypes from Central Asia, known in Italy as *panni tartarici* (Tartar cloth).[57] On either side of the throne are two small angels, dressed in blue and gold, almost identical in shape and pose, each playing a portable organ. Above the throne is a group of sixteen angels (two of whom are covered up by other angels and indicated only by their haloes), all richly clothed and, except for the three central ones, singing and playing musical instruments. The instruments include, from left to right, a frame drum, straight trumpet, mandora, bladder-pipe, vielle, psaltery, lute, shawm, harp-shaped psaltery, straight trumpet, and shawm.[58] Towering over the center of the panel are the figures of Christ and the Virgin seated on the same throne and wearing mantles in blue and silver over red-and-gold tunics. With his right foot over the golden sun, Christ, as King of Heaven, holds a scepter in his left hand. Crowned himself, he places a second crown over the head of his mother, at his side, who tilts her head slightly, accepting the crown, her hands crossed across her chest. The Virgin's feet are placed on an image of the moon, originally more vibrantly colored in silver leaf.

The subject of the Coronation of the Virgin as Queen of Heaven—which started to be represented in Italy in the late thirteenth century—comes not from the Bible but from apocryphal sources. The symbolism of the sun and moon in association with Christ and the Virgin was related to the passage in Revelation 12:1 about the vision in heaven of "a woman clothed with the sun, and the moon under her feet, and upon her a crown of twelve stars." While the apocalyptic vision was usually connected with an image of the Church, both Bonaventure (1221–1274) and the text of the *Speculum humanae salvationis* directly connect the "woman" in Revelation with the Virgin Mary.[59] In early Italian paintings, the scene follows two typologies, either with Christ actively

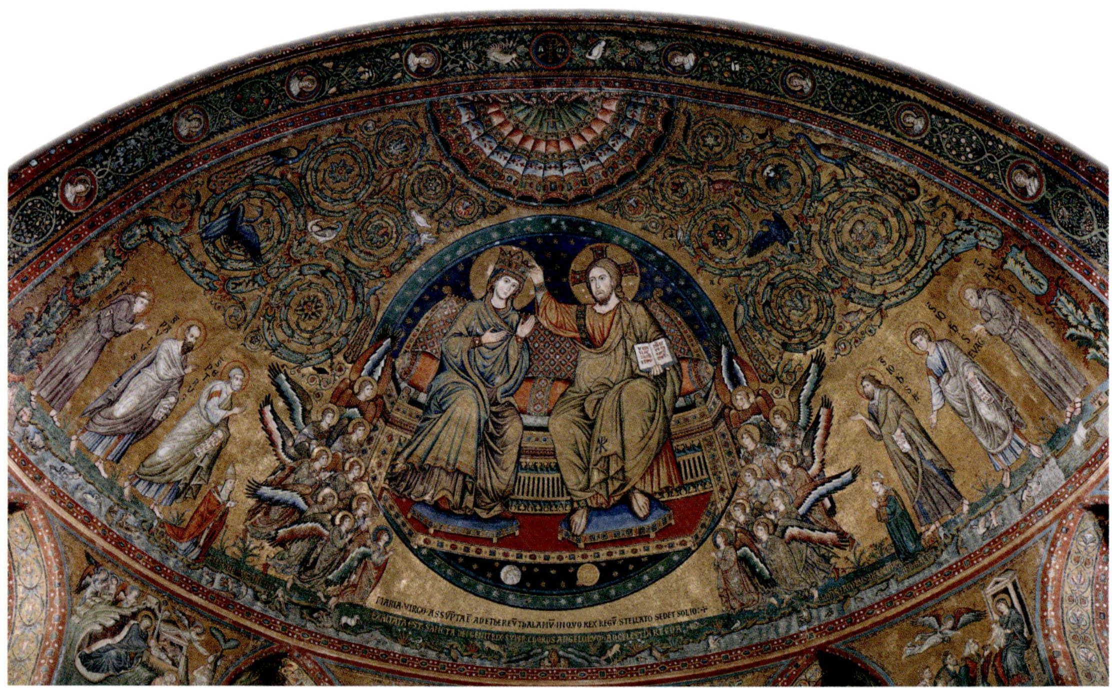

Fig. 13
Jacopo Torriti
Coronation of the Virgin and Saints, 1295
Mosaic
Santa Maria Maggiore, Rome

Fig. 14
Master of the Washington Coronation
The Coronation of the Virgin, 1324
Tempera on panel
45⅜ × 33⅞ in. (115.3 × 86 cm)
National Gallery of Art, Washington

crowning his mother (as in Paolo's works) or with him blessing her after having crowned her. The subject was popular in Venice, as well as Tuscany, and, according to Meiss, it is "not impossible that the Tuscan painters of our period were attracted by Venetian painting of the fourteenth century, as they certainly were by the earlier Byzantinesque art of the Dugento."[60]

One of the earliest depictions of the Coronation of the Virgin in Italy is the monumental apse mosaic in the basilica of Santa Maria Maggiore in Rome, by Jacopo Torriti (fig. 13). Christ is shown crowning his mother, as they both sit on the same throne, with the sun and moon under their feet. They are surrounded by a glory of angels and are flanked by six saints—Francis of Assisi, Paul, and Peter (on the left) and John the Baptist, John the Evangelist, and Anthony of Padua (on the right)—and two kneeling donors—Pope Nicholas IV (1227–1292) and Cardinal Jacopo Colonna (ca. 1250–1318), the archpriest of the basilica. How this visual model reached Venice is uncertain, but Venetian images of the subject followed Torriti's general archetype. The Master of the Washington Coronation—possibly identifiable as Paolo's father, Martino, or his brother, Marco—painted one of the earliest panels of the subject in Venice (fig. 14).[61] As in Torriti's mosaic, Christ and the Virgin sit on a sausage-shaped cushion, with a Cloth of Honor behind them. The throne is surrounded by eight neatly lined-up angels, one above the other and most holding scepters.

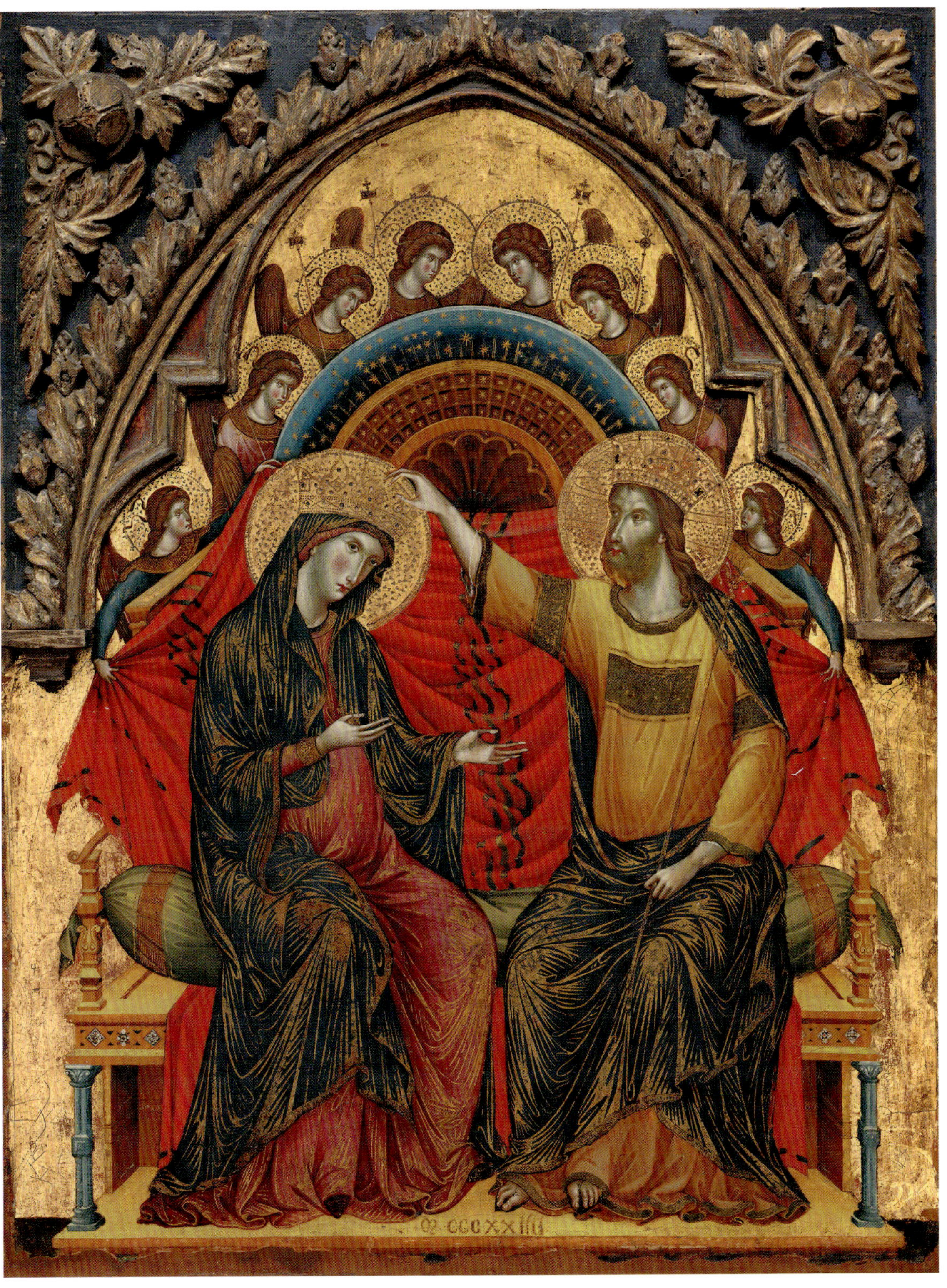
M CCCXXIIII

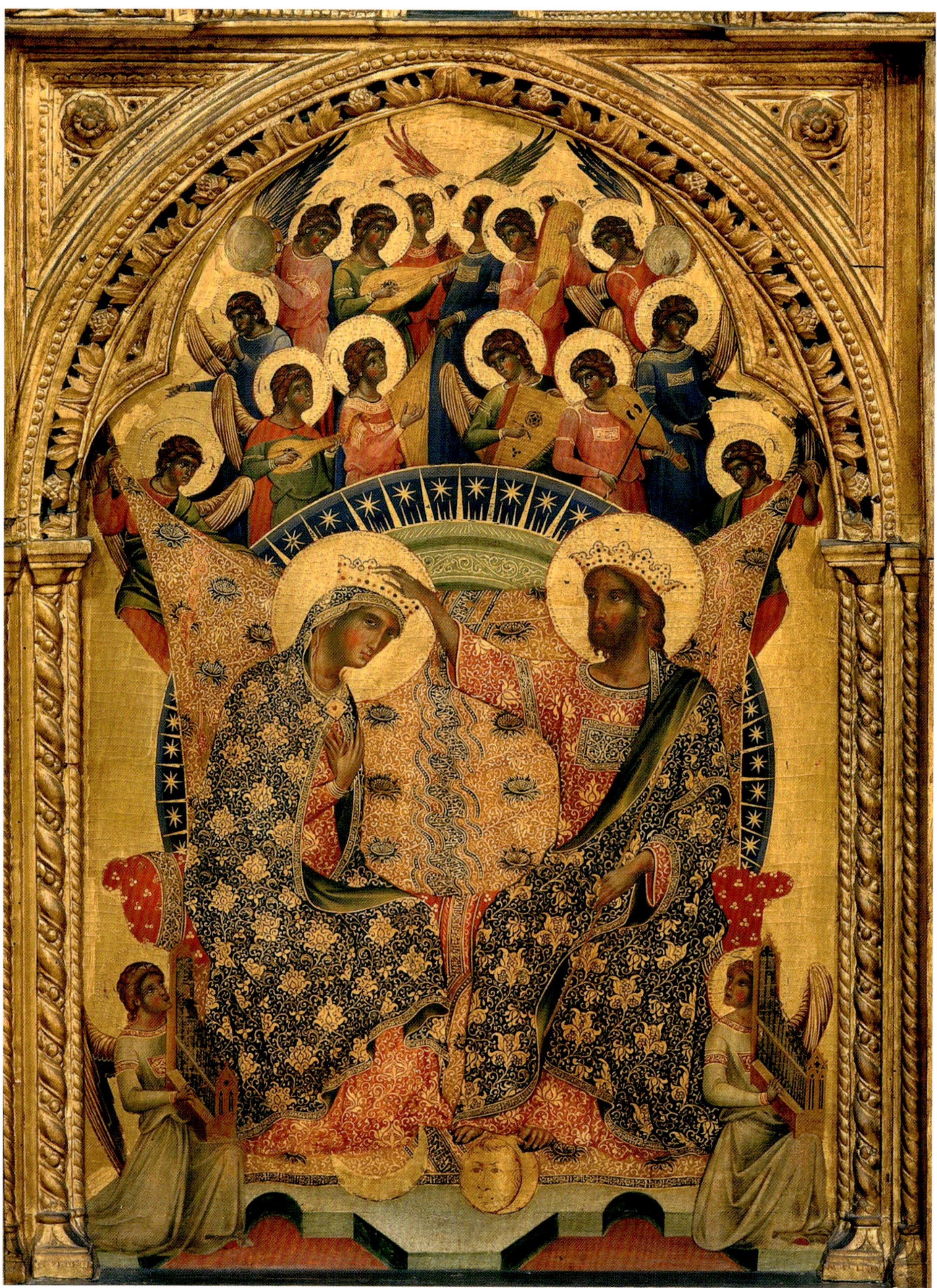

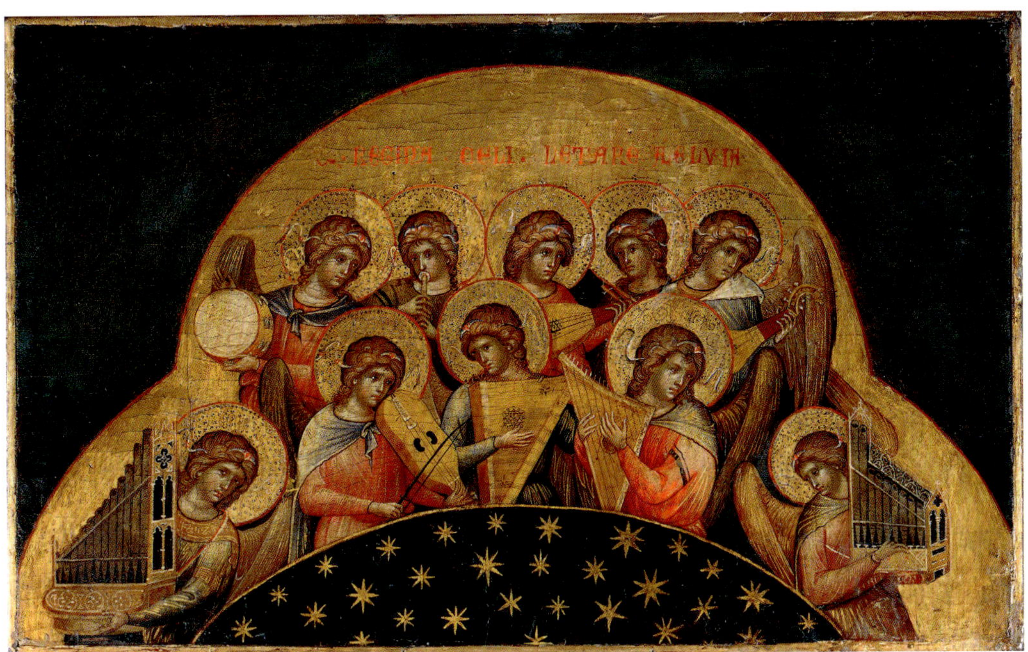

Fig. 15
Paolo Veneziano
Coronation of the Virgin (detail of central compartment of the *Santa Chiara Polyptych*), ca. 1335
Tempera on panel
39⅝ × 25⅛ in. (100.7 × 63.8 cm)
Gallerie dell'Accademia, Venice

Fig. 16
Paolo Veneziano
Choir of Angels (fragment of a lost *Coronation of the Virgin*),
ca. 1340s
Tempera on panel
15$\frac{3}{16}$ × 24 in. (38.5 × 61 cm)
Museo di Palazzo Venezia, Rome

Paolo, who surely knew the work of the Master of the Washington Coronation, painted the Coronation of the Virgin a number of times before his final representation of the subject in the Frick painting. His first known painting of this subject is the central compartment of the Santa Chiara Polyptych (fig. 15), in the mid-1330s. The composition is similar to the one in the Washington painting but with additional details: the sun and the moon (which the Master of the Washington Coronation had not included), the two side angels with portable organs, and nineteen music-making and singing angels behind the throne. Paolo seems to be the first to include a musical component in the iconography of the Coronation, adding both a visual element, with the extraordinary depiction of draperies and textiles, and an auditory one, by providing imagined celestial music as a soundtrack to the painting. The Frick's *Coronation* represents the ultimate development of the Santa Chiara formal composition—its figures more elongated and elegant, the throne more architecturally grand, and the angels assembling above the scene in a denser composition. In the more than twenty years between the two works, Paolo and his workshop produced a number of works with this iconography. A fragment of a panel, showing ten music-making angels, surmounted by the inscription .REGINA. CELI. LETARE. ALELVIA. (Queen of Heaven, rejoice, hallelujah) (fig. 16), is, most likely, a fragment of another *Coronation of the Virgin* by Paolo's workshop from the 1340s.[62]

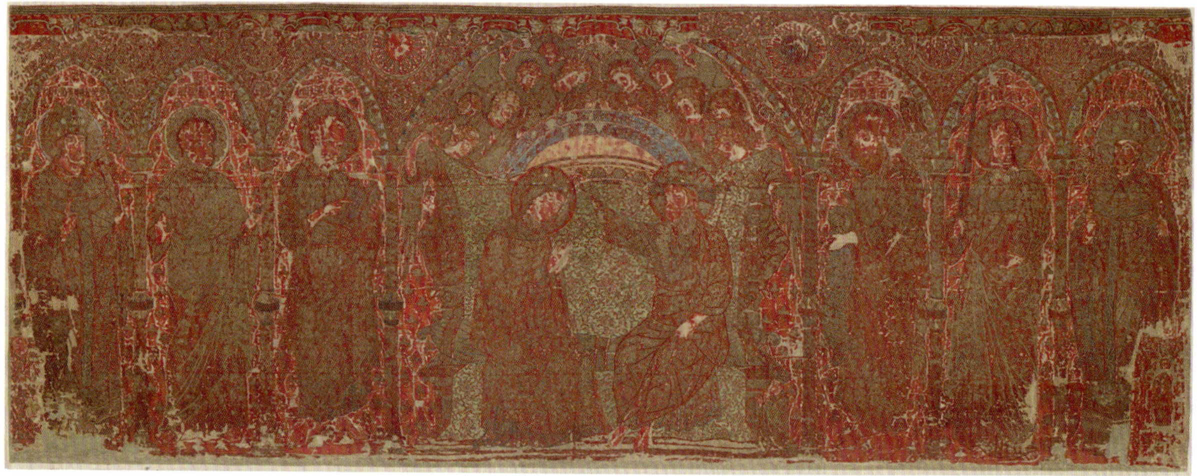

Fig. 17
After Paolo Veneziano
Veglia Altar Frontal, ca. 1330
Red silk, in plain weave; with embroidery of gold and silver threads underside-couched, and with colored silks, mainly in split stitch; interlined with paper and lined with linen
42⅛ × 109⅛ in. (107 × 277 cm)
Victoria and Albert Museum, London

Fig. 18
Donato and Catarino
Coronation of the Virgin, 1372
Tempera on panel
53¹⁵⁄₁₆ × 30⁵⁄₁₆ in. (137 × 77 cm)
Fondazione Querini Stampalia, Venice

The design for the scene was also used by Paolo's workshop in embroidered textiles, which served as altar frontals. Two examples from Croatia—one from the Cathedral of Krk (Veglia) (fig. 17) and another from Dobrinj (Dobrigno)—were *antependia* (coverings hung over the front of altars).[63] In both cases, the central scenes of the Coronation are flanked by standing saints (as in the Santa Maria Maggiore mosaic). In Krk, saints Quirinus, Peter, and John the Evangelist appear on the left of the Coronation, and saints John the Baptist, Paul, and Gaudentius on the right. The Dobrinj textile is a fragment of a larger piece and is now flanked by only two saints: James and Stephen. A number of similar altar frontals with a central Coronation of the Virgin were produced in the fourteenth century in Florence but also as far away as Lower Saxony and Bohemia.[64]

The popularity of the subject of the Coronation certainly continued after Paolo's death. A panel signed by the painters Donato and Catarino and dated 1372 (fig. 18) is clearly based on the prototypes established by Paolo and his workshop in the first half of the century. While the elegance of the figures looks to the Frick *Coronation*, the decoration of the draperies and the general monumentality of the painting relates more closely to Paolo's earlier Santa Chiara *Coronation*. The importance of the theme of the Coronation in Venice reached its peak in 1365, only a few years after Paolo's death, when the Paduan painter Guariento di Arpo (1310–1370) frescoed the scene, surrounded by a vision of Paradise, on the main wall of the principal public space of the Doge's Palace, the Sala del Maggior Consiglio.[65]

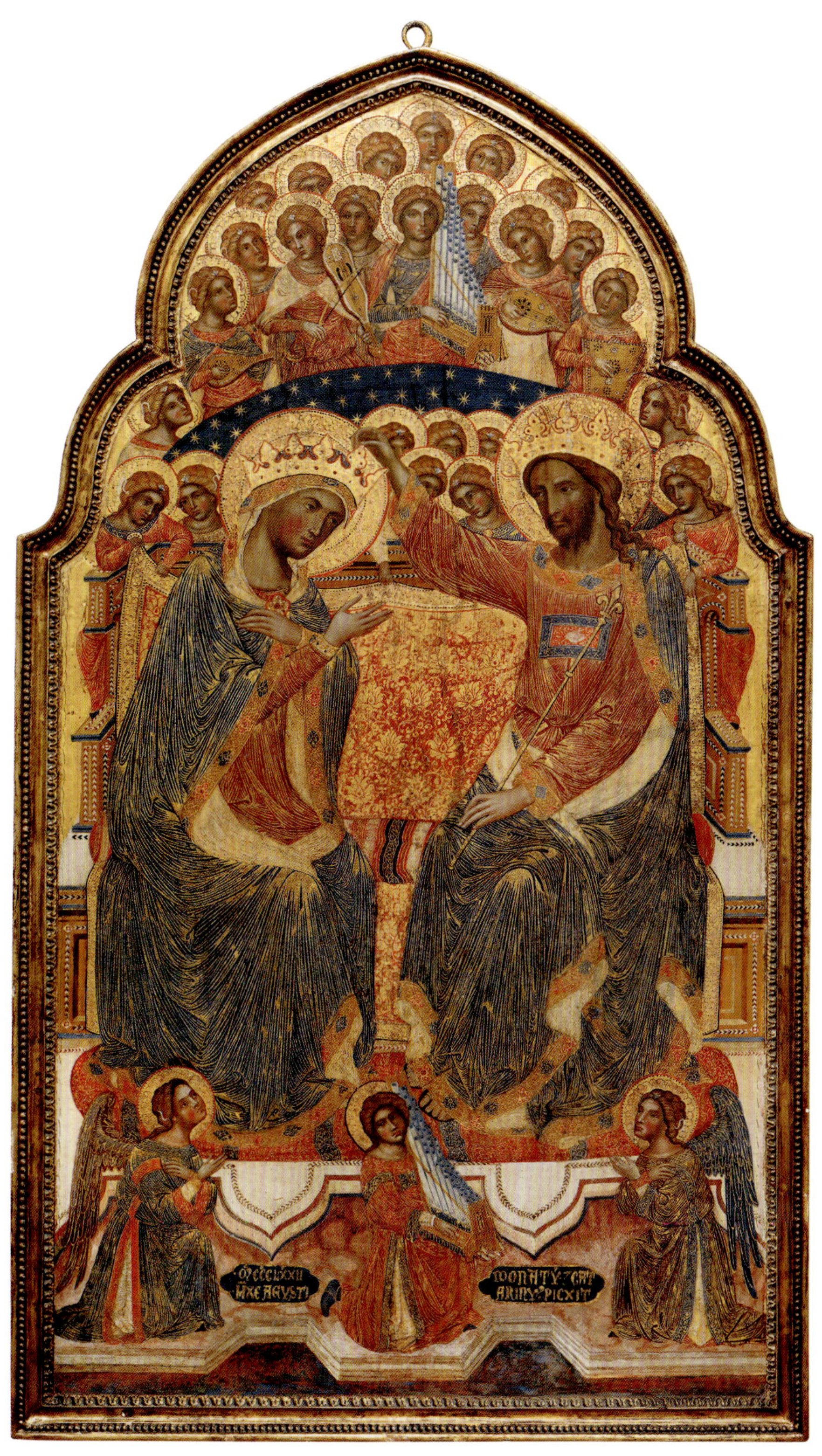
MCCCLXXII
MXE AGVSTI
DONATV ET CAT
ARINV PICXIT

The History of the Frick's *Coronation of the Virgin*

Helen Clay Frick (1888–1984), daughter of the museum's founder, Henry Clay Frick (1849–1919), was particularly fond of early Italian art. She traveled extensively across the Italian Peninsula, and, as her interest was mostly in the Italian school of painting that flourished in central Italy, she often went to Tuscany and Umbria. On July 12–13, 1925, while staying at the Grand Hotel in Venice, she wrote in her diary, "Venice was too full of Germans, so that I longed to be away in peaceful Tuscany!"[66] She did not write about any works by Paolo Veneziano on this brief Venetian visit, instead focusing on a painter of the next generation, Lorenzo Veneziano (act. 1356–72): "I was charmed with Lorenzo Veneziano who, perhaps because of his Byzantine character and early coloring & feeling, is very reminiscent of the Sienese School."[67] In addition to her diaries, Helen kept notebooks, most of which focused on Tuscan painting (and especially Sienese), but she also collected information on Venetian artists. In one of these notebooks, probably compiled in the 1920s, she recorded information on "Maestro Paolo, the earliest personality in Venetian painting."[68] She wrote about three of his works: the Vicenza *Dormition of the Virgin*, the *Virgin and Child* at the Louvre, and *The Coronation of the Virgin*. Helen astutely described the painting: "typical Venetian representation of the angels piled up, and the types, little by little, more Venetian (i.e., Christ's large forehead narrowing at the eyes and narrow in the lower part. Eyes with curious expression, hands, thin and small)." Showing her Tuscan bias, she related the painting to Florentine art: "signed and dated 1358. (Almost the same date as the Nardo di Cione in S. M. Novella)." But she also wrote that "Dr. [Richard] Offner considers this his master-piece."

Helen described *The Coronation of the Virgin* as being in the gallery at Sigmaringen, in Germany. By the late 1920s, the painting was in the hands of M. Knoedler & Co., the art dealer that for fifty years had been selling paintings to Helen's father. Knoedler also produced for potential buyers a booklet on the painting, which outlined its known history and cited a number of published descriptions.[69] The painting was sent to The Frick Collection for inspection by the trustees on March 6 and again on April 18, 1929.[70] Helen must have asked for the opinion of Richard Offner (1889–1965), one of the most important art historians working on early Italian paintings in the United States at the time, as he wrote a one-page appreciation of the painting, on March 4, 1929:

> [The panel] combines the mystery of Northern grace with Eastern gravity, a Gothic gaiety with Oriental splendour, to a harmony so vital that we do not know whether the brilliant colour recalls Persian painting or its spirit, French miniatures. The fusion of these two elements runs throughout the picture; for the main figures are French in type as much as the scene is Byzantine in its presentation, and in its technique; and again the informal conduct of the angels is as Northern European as the main action is Greek.

Offner concluded, "The picture is no less rare as a monument, not only on account of the final authentication in the signature, and the date, but also because of its uncommonly good state." Among the other collectors from whom Helen sought advice was her father's good friend Andrew W. Mellon (1855–1937), one of the founders of the National Gallery in Washington and at that time Secretary of the Treasury. On February 8, 1930, Mellon wrote:

> My dear Helen:
> I received your letter of January 24th and have delayed sending you a reply until I could be certain whether I might be going to New York and could view the painting of "The Coronation of the Virgin" by Paola [sic!] Veneziano, which is under consideration as an addition to The Frick Collection.
>
> I hope to do so in the near future and am writing now to say that I have been favorably impressed by the photograph of the painting. I am not familiar with the work of this painter but it is possible that the picture would be an excellent addition to the Collection.

The painting was eventually sent to Washington for inspection by Mellon, who wrote to Helen on March 10: "I thought it a beautiful painting, of fine execution, and in unusually good condition. The price asked, $190,000, seems to me quite reasonable considering present day values. . . . I feel justified in recommending it and feel sure that you will make no mistake in acquiring it at the price mentioned." With Mellon's approval, Helen solicited the opinions of the Frick's trustees: George F. Baker Jr. (1840–1931), Horace Havemeyer (1886–1956), and John D. Rockefeller Jr. (1874–1960). Havemeyer replied, "While it is a picture that does not make much of a personal appeal to me, nevertheless, I consider it worthy of a place in the Frick Collection." In late March, Rockefeller inspected the painting, subsequently describing it as "beautiful and well painted." But while it gave him "much pleasure," he found one feature "a little disturbing"—"the fresh, crude and rather hard

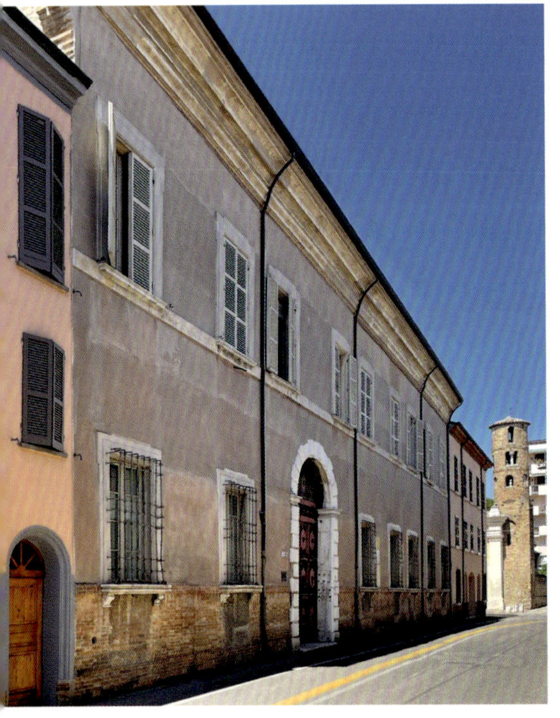

and obtruding character of the architecture of the bench upon which the two figures are seated." Nonetheless, he concluded, "I am quite willing to cast my vote for the purchase of the painting." In April 1930, the board approved the purchase, and, on the twenty-sixth of that month, the museum acquired the painting for $190,000. It was a bold and important acquisition at a time when the Frick was building its collection of Italian gold-ground works and Paolo Veneziano was not well represented in American museums.[71] Only a few years before, in 1927, the Worcester Art Museum in Massachusetts had purchased works by Paolo—the *Seven Saints* originally part of a small devotional triptych. To this day, the Frick's *Coronation* remains the most important piece by Paolo in an American museum, even though other smaller panels by him have subsequently been acquired by other institutions.

When Knoedler purchased the *Coronation* from the German dealer A. S. Drey, it had been in Germany for more than sixty years.[72] In a lecture at the Münchener Alterthums-Vereins, the Antiquarians' Association, in Munich on February 25, 1867, the art dealer Joseph Maillinger (1831–1884) discussed "a painting in his possession by master Paolo Veneziano dated 1358."[73] In his lecture, Maillinger tried to reconstruct the career of Paolo, with a list of works and dates, and, when a transcript of the lecture was published, the *Coronation of the Virgin* was illustrated for the first time. In 1869, Maillinger lent the panel to a public show in the exhibition building across from the Glyptothek (Kunstausstellungsgebäude gegenüber der Glyptothek).[74] Among the art historians who saw it there were Giovanni Battista Cavalcaselle (1819–1897) and Joseph Archer Crowe (1825–1896), who subsequently described it in detail in one of their publications.[75]

Fig. 19
Palazzo Bacinetti, Ravenna

Fig. 20
Interior with frescos by Felice Giani, Palazzo Bacinetti, Ravenna

There is no documentation of Paolo's *Coronation of the Virgin* before Maillinger's lecture in 1867. Maillinger claimed that the "origin of the painting" was "a chapel near Ravenna, now used as a coal store."[76] Neither the referenced chapel nor its location is known. According to later sources, the *Coronation* belonged to "a count Baccinetti before belonging to Maillinger,"[77] though it is not known where this information came from. The Bacinetti were a prominent aristocratic family in Ravenna, and the count referred to

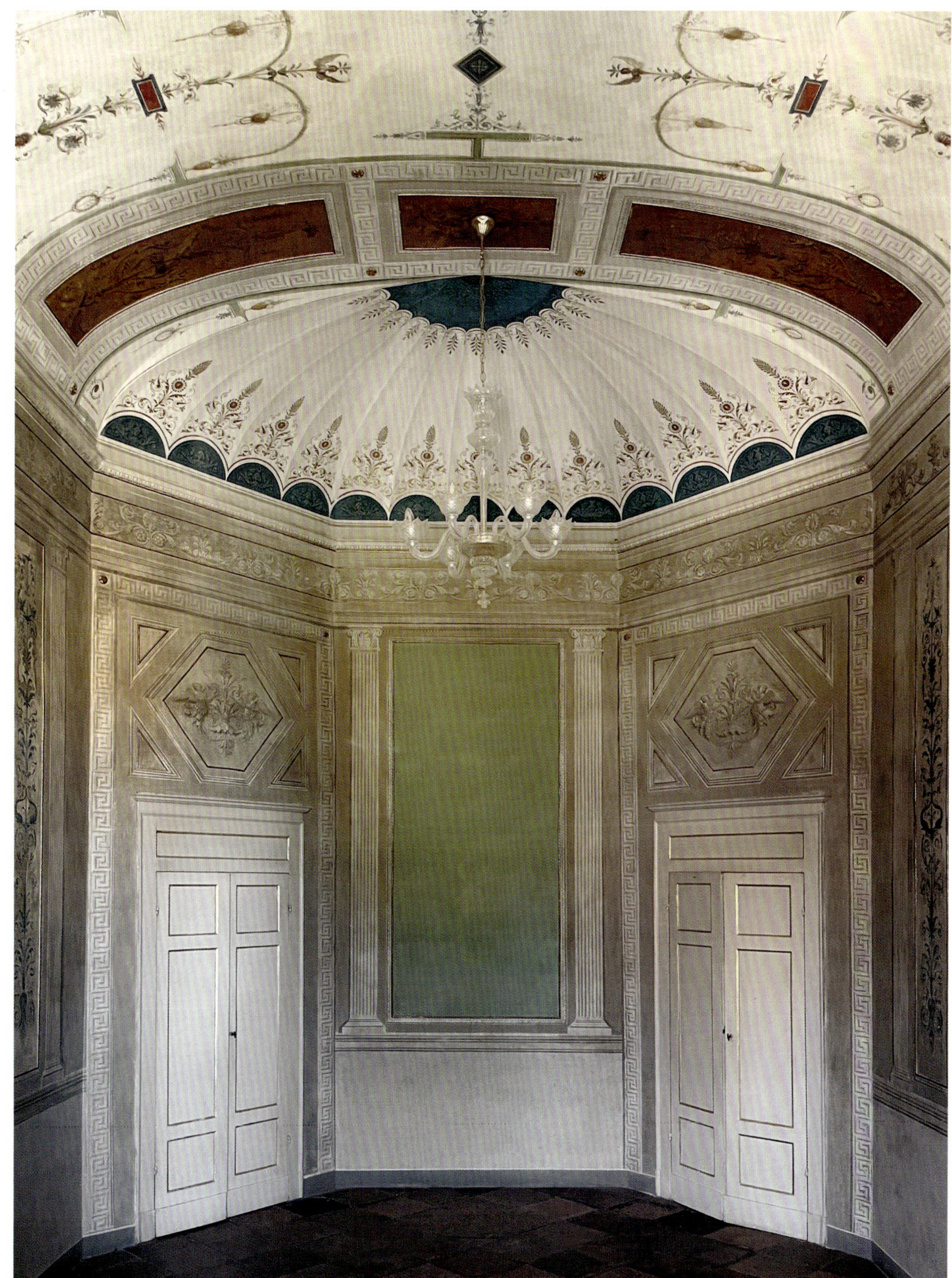

Fig. 21
Bertel Thorvaldsen
Marianna Bacinetti Florenzi, 1858
Marble, h. 29⁵⁄₁₆ in. (74.4 cm)
Thorvaldsen Museum, Copenhagen

is likely Pietro Bacinetti (1771–1819), who lived in Ravenna between the end of the eighteenth and the first half of the nineteenth century.[78] The Bacinetti had two palazzi in Ravenna, one of which (fig. 19) was restored in the eighteenth century by the Camaldolese architect Giuseppe Antonio Soratini (1682–1762) and later decorated with neoclassical frescos by Felice Giani (1758–1823) (fig. 20).[79] It is not known in which of the two palazzi the *Coronation* was likely displayed as part of a larger collection of paintings, of which—at present—nothing is known.

A link not previously explored may shed some light on how the painting reached Germany from Ravenna. Bacinetti's daughter, Marianna (1802–1870) (fig. 21), was well known in Italy at the time.[80] She was not only a great beauty but also a keen student of philosophy who translated Friedrich Wilhelm Joseph Schelling's (1775–1854) *Bruno* (1844) from the original German into Italian. She was a staunch supporter of Italian independence and published a number of controversial volumes and pamphlets between 1850 and 1868: *Confutazione del socialismo e comunismo* (Rebuttal on Socialism and Communism), *Saggi di psicologia e logica* (Essays in Psychology and Logic), *L'Austria in relazione all'Italia* (Austria in Relation to Italy), *Sulle cose attuali d'Italia* (On the Present Situation of Italy), and *Dell'immortalità dell'anima umana* (On the Immortality of the Human Soul). Marianna was married twice: first to Marquis Ettore Florenzi of Perugia in 1819, and in 1836—after Florenzi's death in 1833—to the Englishman Evelyn Waddington, who would later be mayor of Perugia. Most noteworthy, however, was Marianna's relationship with Prince Ludwig of Bavaria (1786–1868), later King Ludwig I, whom she met during Carnival in Rome in 1821 and with whom she subsequently traveled to Munich. She and the king were most likely lovers for the next several decades. Marianna had a son, Ludovico Florenzi (1821–1896)—no doubt Ludwig's child—who was the king's godchild. Though not demonstrable through documentary sources, it is likely that Paolo's *Coronation of the Virgin* passed from Ravenna to Munich through Marianna, who may have inherited it from her father, Pietro, and then sold it to Maillinger, before Ludwig's death.[81] Marianna also had three brothers—Girolamo (b. 1804), Giuseppe (b. 1806), and Luigi (b. 1814)—and three sisters—Maria Teresa (b. 1805), Olimpia (b. 1808), and Virginia (b. 1811).[82] The family's financial situation seems to have been precarious, and this may well have been the reason for the sale of the painting and possibly of the entire Bacinetti collection of works of art.

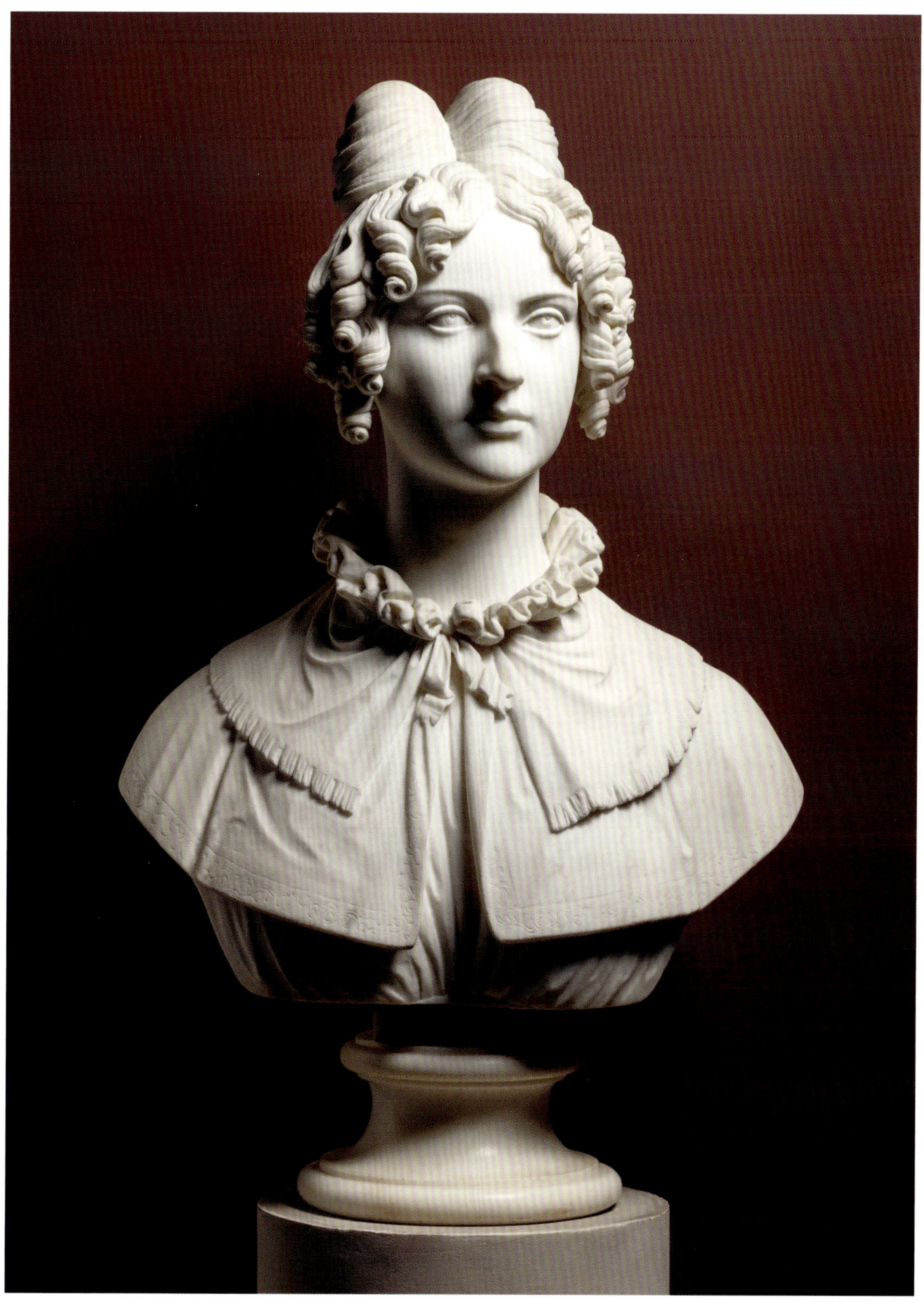

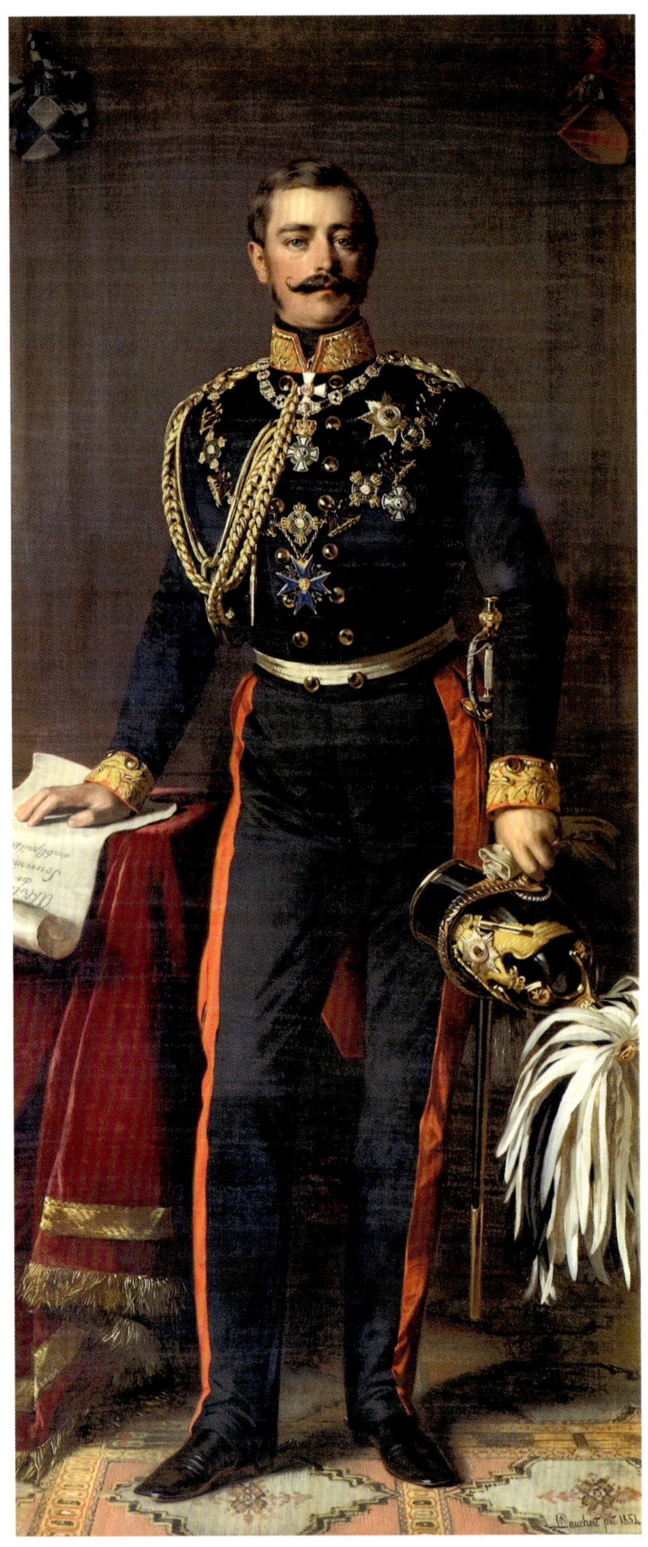

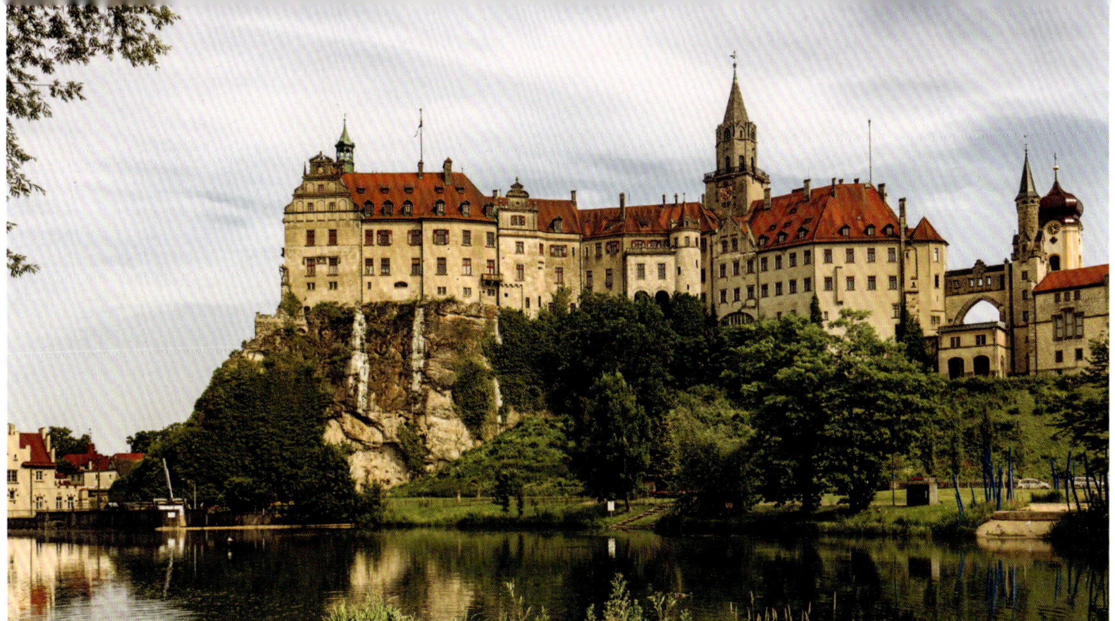

By 1873, the *Coronation* was owned by the Munich painter Franz Reichardt (1825–1887). That same year, the painting was purchased by Prince Karl Anton von Hohenzollern-Sigmaringen (1811–1885) (fig. 22), whereupon it entered the collection of the family castle at Sigmaringen (fig. 23).[83] The prince had assembled more than two hundred paintings in the castle—mostly German and Dutch but also more than twenty Italian paintings, of which Paolo's *Coronation* was the most important.[84] The collection was housed in a gallery and two other rooms, built in 1862.[85] The picture gallery existed alongside the castle's armory, library, and medals cabinet. In 1867, the paintings were installed in these spaces, which were opened to the public as a museum on October 5 of that year. In 1893, the art historian Fritz Harck wrote, "The Sigmaringen collection is virtually a German Museo Poldi-Pezzoli," drawing an interesting link between the German castle and the Milanese museum, which was later one of the inspirations behind the creation of such American museums as the Isabella Stewart Gardner Museum in Boston and The Frick Collection in New York.[86] Paolo's *Coronation* remained at Sigmaringen for fifty-five years—through four generations of the princely Hohenzollern-Sigmaringen family. The castle and the collection were inherited by Prince Karl Anton's son Leopold (1835–1905) and grandson Wilhelm (1864–1927). In the fall of 1928, his son Frederick (1891–1965)—Karl Anton's great-grandson—exhibited a number of paintings from Sigmaringen, including the Paolo Veneziano, at the Alte Pinakothek in Munich.[87] Soon after that, he dispersed the collection, and the Paolo panel was sold in 1928, passing to the dealer A. S. Drey.[88] Two years later, the painting was purchased by the Frick.

Fig. 22
Richard Lauchert
Prince Karl Anton von Hohenzollern-Sigmaringen, 1854
Oil on canvas
87⅜ × 35⅜ in. (222 × 90 cm)
Princely Hohenzollern Collections

Fig. 23
Castle of Sigmaringen

The San Severino Polyptych

From 1867, when Maillinger mentioned *The Coronation of the Virgin* in his lecture, to 1930, when the panel was purchased by the Frick, Paolo's painting was believed to be an independent work of art, as is the case for a number of his other panels. However, notwithstanding the fact that not a single large work by him survives in its entirety, most of his identified paintings are now known to have originally been part of much larger ensembles. *The Coronation of the Virgin* at the center of the Santa Chiara Polyptych gives a good idea of

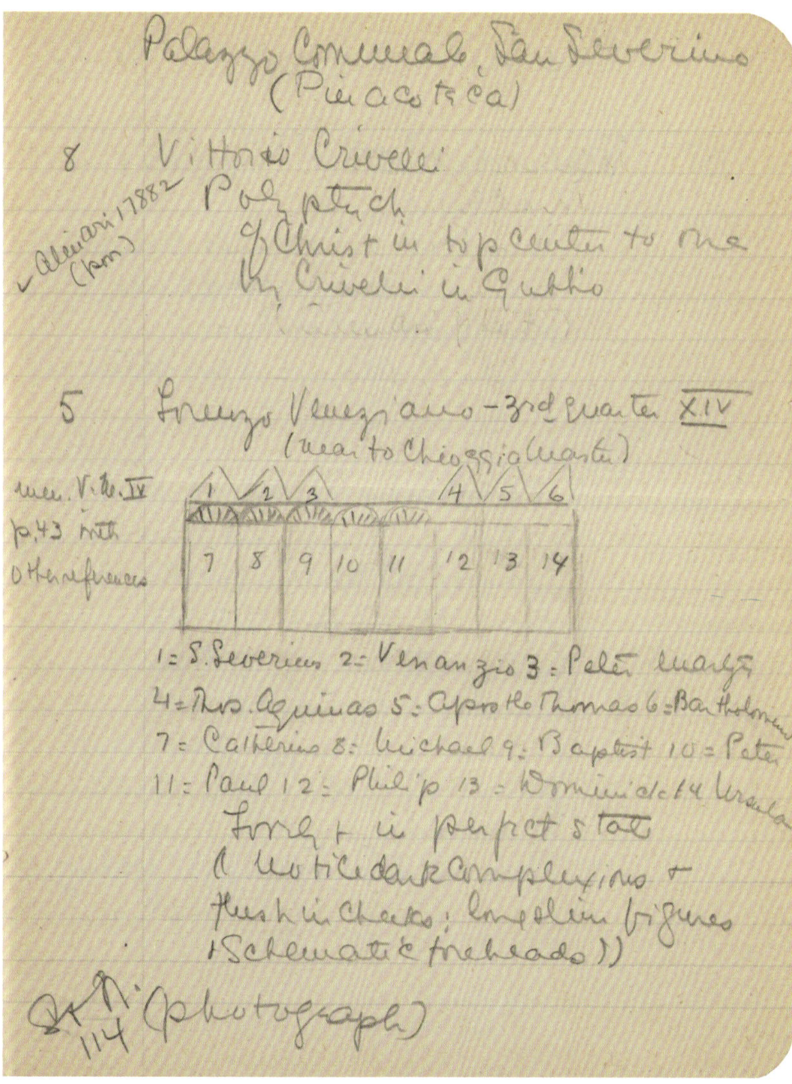

Palazzo Comunale, San Severino
(Pinacoteca)

8 Vittorio Crivelli
Polyptych
of Christ in top center to one
by Crivelli in Gubbio

✓ Alinari 17882

5 Lorenzo Veneziano – 3rd quarter XIV
(near to Chioggia master)

Ven. V. IV p. 43 with other references

1	2	3			4	5	6
7	8	9	10	11	12	13	14

1 = S. Severinus 2 = Venanzio 3 = Peter Martyr
4 = Thos. Aquinas 5 = Apostle Thomas 6 = Bartholomew
7 = Catherine 8 = Michael 9 = Baptist 10 = Peter
11 = Paul 12 = Philip 13 = Dominic 14 = Ursula
Lovely + in perfect state
(Note the dark complexions + flush in cheeks; long slim figures (schematic foreheads))

114 (photograph)

Fig. 24 (overleaf)
Paolo and Giovanni Veneziano
Fourteen Saints, 1358
Tempera on panel
66 15/16 × 105½ in. (170 × 268 cm)
Pinacoteca Comunale Padre Tacchi Venturi, San Severino Marche

Fig. 25
Helen Clay Frick, Sketch of Paolo and Giovanni Veneziano's *Fourteen Saints* in the Pinacoteca of San Severino Marche, 1925
The Frick Collection/Frick Art Reference Library Archives, New York

how works like the Frick *Coronation* must have once stood at the center of important altarpieces. Surprisingly, it was not until the Frick's paintings were fully catalogued, in 1968, that Bernice Davidson suggested that Paolo's panel was "almost certainly . . . originally part of a polyptych, flanked, as in many examples, by smaller narrative scenes or attendant saints."[89]

On July 19, 1925, five years before the *Coronation*'s acquisition by the Frick, Helen Clay Frick traveled to the small town of San Severino in the Marche.[90] There—after having looked at art in Urbino, Gubbio, and Fabriano and before heading to Camerino—she visited the Pinacoteca, where she was struck by the fragments of a polyptych showing eight standing saints and six other half-length saints on the upper register (fig. 24). Helen described the paintings, which were then attributed to Lorenzo Veneziano, as "lovely & in perfect state." She sketched and annotated a scheme of the panels in her notebook, identifying the saints (fig. 25), and, in one of her travel scrapbooks, included a black-and-white photograph of the work (fig. 26). Long attributed to Lorenzo Veneziano, the San Severino panels were officially returned to the correct authorship of Paolo in 1930 by Evelyn

Fig. 26
Photograph of Paolo and Giovanni Veneziano's *Fourteen Saints* in the Pinacoteca of San Severino Marche, in Helen Clay Frick's Travel Scrapbook, 1925
The Frick Collection/Frick Art Reference Library Archives, New York

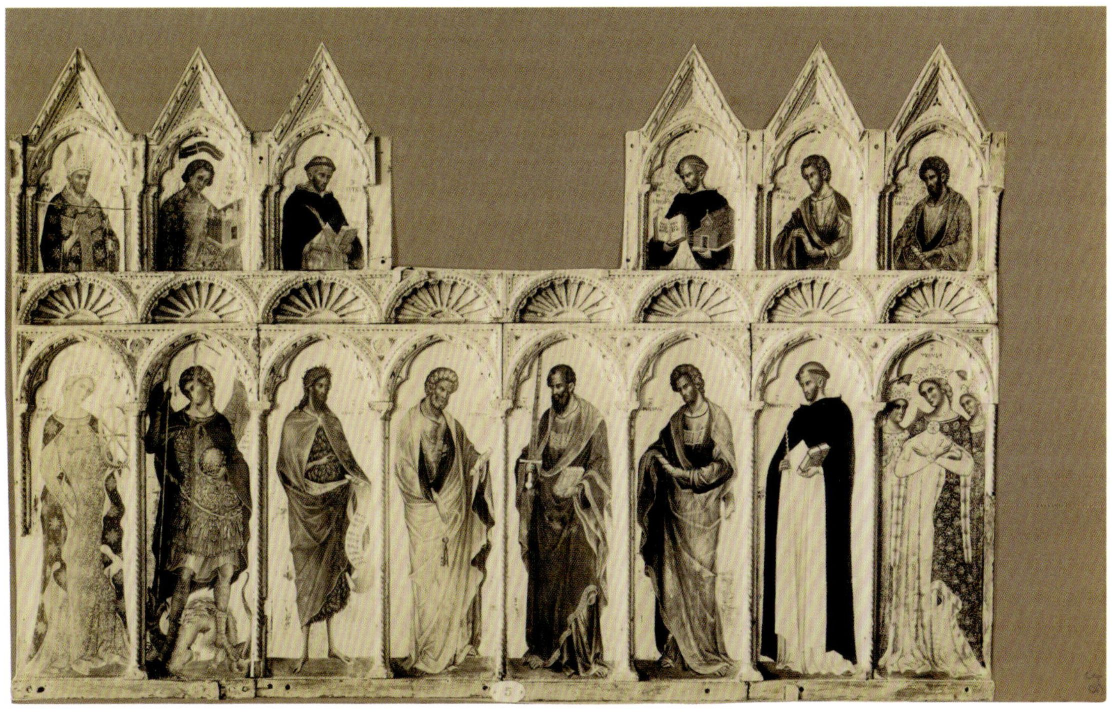

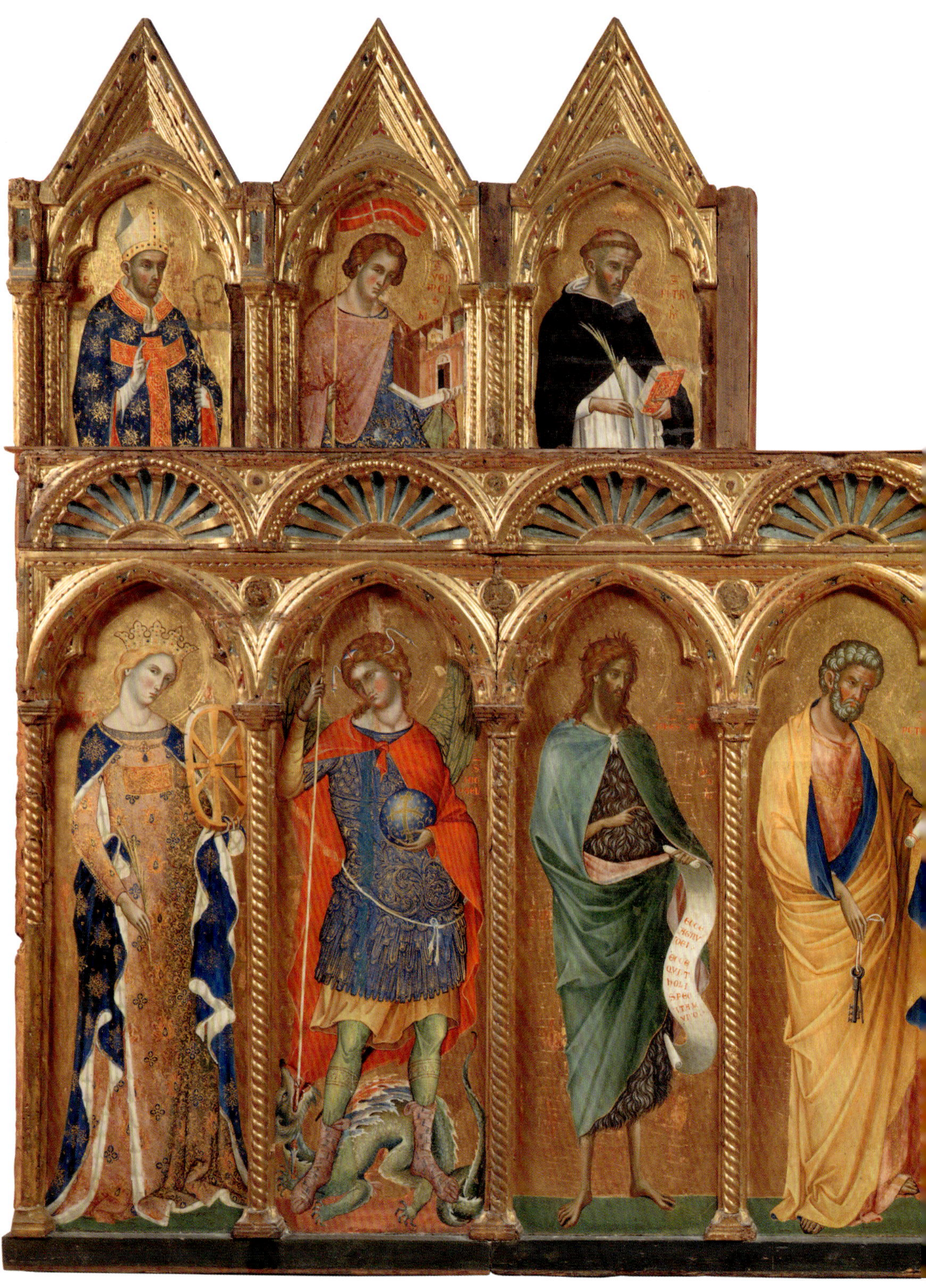

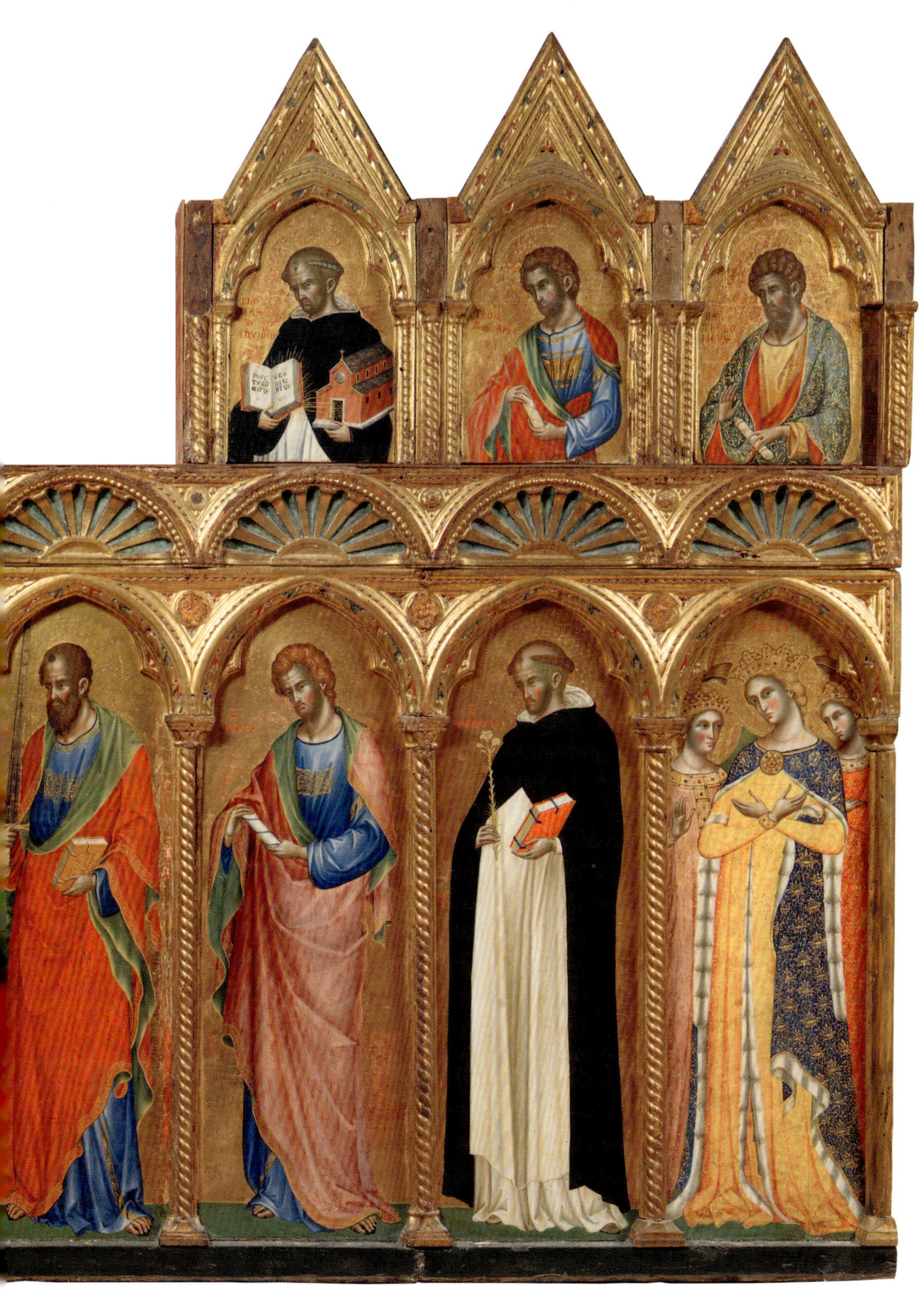

Sandberg Vavalà, in one of the first scholarly articles outlining the career and oeuvre of the artist.[91] Coincidentally, the article was published just as the Frick was acquiring Paolo's *Coronation*. The questions regarding the origins of the painting became linked with the study of the San Severino *Fourteen Saints* only twenty years later, when Rodolfo Pallucchini, in 1950, remarked on a stylistic affinity between the two works: "that the complex of figures in the San Severino Polyptych . . . is close to the Frick *Coronation* seems evident."[92] However, Pallucchini did not go any further with this. Not until 1977 did the German scholar Hanna Kiel, writing in the journal *Pantheon*, brilliantly connect the Frick *Coronation* and the San Severino panels and suggest the reconstruction of a single polyptych.[93]

Like the Frick *Coronation*, the San Severino panels are not documented until the early nineteenth century.[94] In 1820, paintings in the sacristy of the Dominican church of Santa Maria del Glorioso (fig. 27), just outside the city of San Severino, were noticed by a local historian, Giuseppe Ranaldi (1790–1854).[95] Ranaldi described the panels in detail and attributed them to Allegretto Nuzi (1315–1373), a local artist active in the area around Fabriano, in the Marche. He also recognized that the panels originally formed part of a large polyptych, the central part of which was missing. Since the church of Santa Maria del Glorioso was not built until after 1519, Ranaldi thought it likely that the polyptych was originally in the main Dominican church of the city—Santa Maria del Mercato.[96] Thanks to Ranaldi, the paintings became known to scholars, and, in 1838, Count Severino Servanzi Collio (1796–1891) showed them to the Prussian art historian Johannes Gaye (1804–1840), who was visiting San Severino on February 18–19 of that year.[97] Servanzi Collio wrote that Gaye thought that the paintings "were absolutely not by Allegretto, but by another school. He believes it to be of the old Venetian School."[98]

By 1868, however, the work was missing, as mentioned by Domenico Valentini (1789–1876) in a local guidebook: "It has disappeared, and who stole it remains unknown."[99] Following the unification of Italy, in the early months of 1861, many religious institutions were suppressed and their properties appropriated by the new Kingdom. Like a number of other works in San Severino churches, Paolo's panels were removed and hidden for safekeeping, in his case in the house of a peasant called Bissoni, who used them as a bed screen. Discovered there by a priest, Pacifico Taddei (1824–1906), the panels were taken by a local senator, Carlo Luzi (1818–1899).[100] In 1895, under pressure

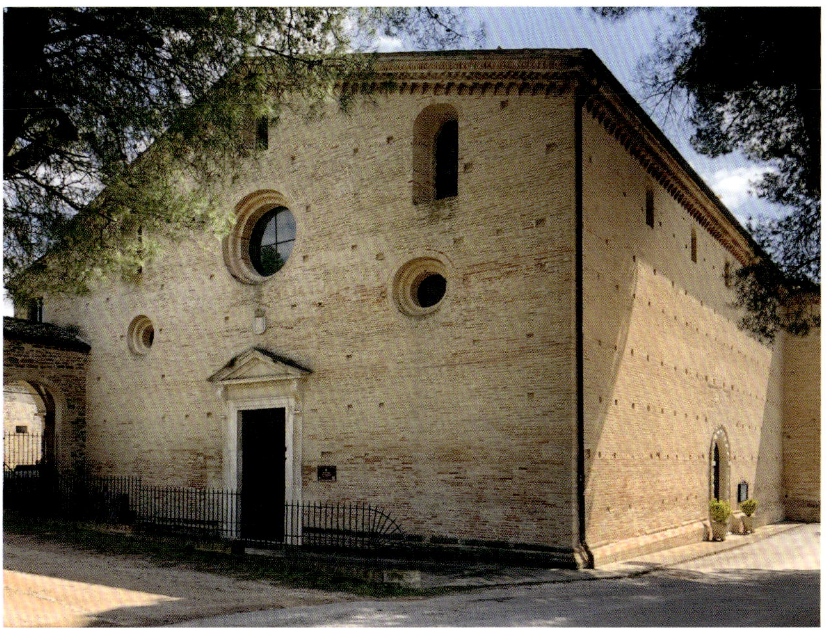

Fig. 27
Santa Maria del Glorioso, San Severino Marche

from the authorities, Luzi returned the work to the city of San Severino, where it was displayed in the Pinacoteca, the newly created civic picture gallery. After its restitution and public display, the curator of the Pinacoteca, Vittorio Emanuele Aleandri (1863–1927), changed the attribution of the work to the Venetian School, specifically to Lorenzo Veneziano, following Gaye's first proposal.[101] It was in the Pinacoteca, and with an attribution to Lorenzo Veneziano, that Helen Clay Frick saw the paintings, in 1925.

The fourteen saints represented in the polyptych, which are still on view at the Pinacoteca, have been reunited to create a single ensemble but originally must have been separated in two parts. On each side of the central panel were four standing, full-length saints, each identified by red inscriptions: Catherine of Alexandria, the Archangel Michael, John the Baptist, and Peter on the left, and, on the right, Paul, Philip, Dominic, and Ursula. Above them were half-length figures of more saints (two of which are missing): Severinus, Venantius, and Peter Martyr on the left, and Thomas Aquinas, Thomas the Apostle, and Bartholomew on the right. The identities of the saints make two things clear: first, the original polyptych must have been created for San Severino, as the presence of the relatively obscure local patron saint would be difficult to explain otherwise; and, second, it must have been commissioned by a Dominican institution because three of the fourteen saints—Dominic, Peter Martyr, and Thomas Aquinas—are Dominican.[102] Examining the history of the San Severino *Fourteen Saints* along with that of the Frick's *Coronation of the Virgin*, Hanna Kiel, in 1977, proposed for the first time that the New York panel was originally the central compartment of the dismembered polyptych, and she provided a reconstruction of the original (fig. 28).[103] Kiel's reconstruction was heavily, and reasonably, based on the two most complete surviving polyptychs by Paolo and his workshop: the Santa Chiara Polyptych in Venice and the San Giacomo Maggiore Polyptych in Bologna. Following the design provided by the remnants of the original frame around the San Severino fragments, Kiel hypothesized that a large shell element surmounted the central *Coronation*, as with the other two polyptychs in Venice and Bologna. She also shifted the six half-length saints toward the center so that the two Dominican saints would be closer to the central image and the missing ones on the external edges. She also proposed that the polyptych was originally painted for the Dominican church of San Severino, Santa Maria del Mercato, something that had been suggested by Giuseppe Ranaldi in 1820. Consecrated in 1304, the church had replaced an older, smaller church on the site, close to the main market square in San Severino.[104] The church was badly damaged in the fifteenth century, especially after a fire in 1428, and was restored and rebuilt a number

Fig. 28
Hanna Kiel's reconstruction of Paolo and Giovanni Veneziano's *San Severino Polyptych*, 1977

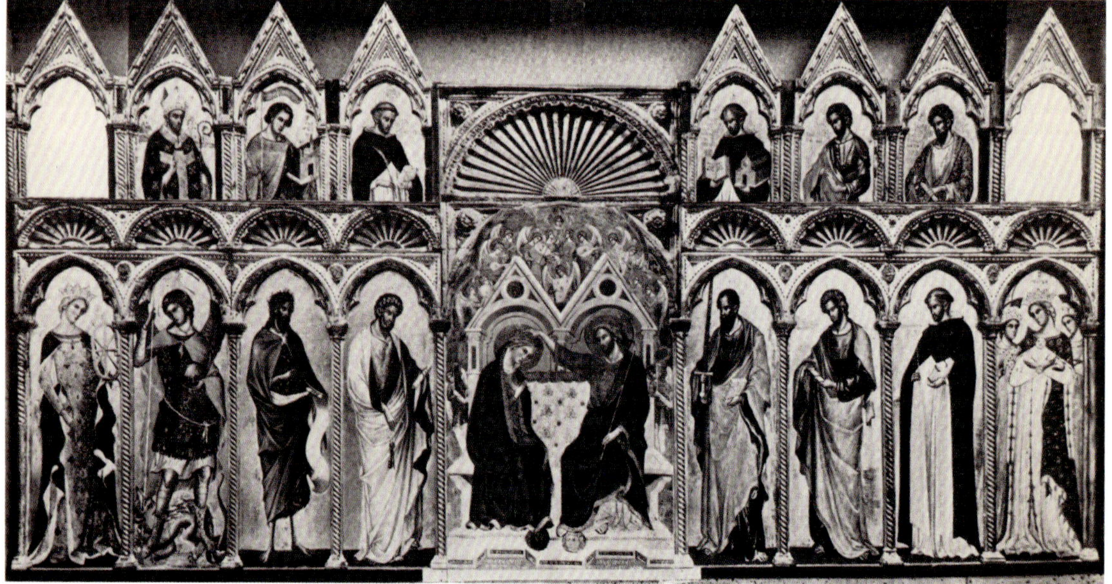

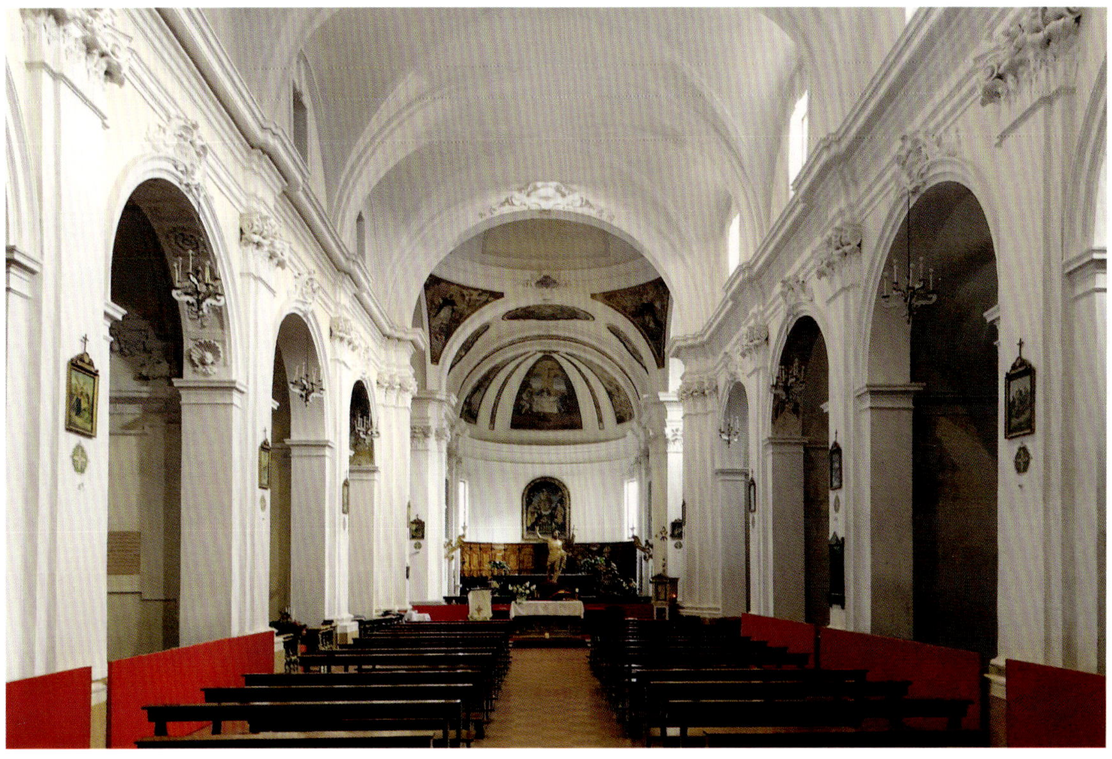

Fig. 29
San Domenico, San Severino Marche

of times, reaching its present form in 1664 (fig. 29). Having belonged to the Dominican order since its creation, the church later changed its name from Santa Maria del Mercato to San Domenico, as it is known today.

Kiel's proposal has been widely accepted by art historians, and it is now generally acknowledged that the San Severino Polyptych was painted in 1358, at the end of Paolo's career, by Paolo and his son Giovanni, most likely for the high altar of Santa Maria del Mercato.[105] *The Coronation of the Virgin* was therefore flanked on each side by two rows of four saints, for a total of sixteen. The gilt decoration on the panels is incredibly rich and consistent across the ensemble, and the figures have the stylistic elongation characteristic of Paolo's later works.[106] The decorative punchwork in the haloes of the San Severino paintings and the Frick panel is also identical, as is the lettering of the various inscriptions across the polyptych. The saints represented, as recently demonstrated by Raoul Paciaroni, were all particularly venerated by the Dominicans at Santa Maria del Mercato, and relics of some of them were among the treasures of the church.[107] One of the most important relics in the

Fig. 30
Gherardo di Jacopo Cavazza
Reliquary for the Hand of St. Philip the Apostle, 1326
Gilded cast copper with engraving and repoussé work; partially gilded punched silver; enamel, gemstones
h. 21¼ in. (54 cm)
Pinacoteca Comunale Padre Tacchi Venturi, San Severino Marche

church was the hand of the apostle Philip, which had been preserved there since at least the mid-thirteenth century.[108] In 1326, the relic was housed in a precious reliquary that was commissioned by the rector of the convent, Francesco Boni, from the goldsmith Gherardo di Jacopo Cavazza from Bologna, who was active at the time in Camerino (fig. 30).[109]

The circumstances under which Paolo received the commission from the Dominicans in San Severino remain unknown. In many ways, this last known polyptych by Paolo is unusual. Of all his surviving works, it would have been the largest. Its original location is also unusual. As far as we know, all Paolo's known paintings were produced for Venice, the Veneto, and cities along the Adriatic coast, but San Severino is located in central Italy, away from the coast. Like many other cities in the Marche region, however, San Severino had important commercial and political links with Venice in the fourteenth century.[110] When and how the polyptych was disassembled is unknown. By the early nineteenth century, the *Coronation* had reached Ravenna, and the side panels in San Severino had been moved to Santa Maria del Glorioso, outside the city's center, and placed in a peripheral location, in the sacristy. By that time, the work of Paolo Veneziano and his workshop had become largely unknown.

A number of questions remain about the reconstruction of the original polyptych. The altarpiece must have had one or more crowning elements, above *The Coronation of the Virgin*, which are now missing. In 2000, Alessandro Marchi proposed that a *Crucifixion* (fig. 31) by Paolo, now in the National Gallery of Victoria in Melbourne, may be the lost cimasa of the San Severino Polyptych (fig. 32).[111] The width of the Melbourne *Crucifixion* is similar to that of the Frick's *Coronation*. However, on stylistic grounds, Marchi's proposal has not met with much favor among scholars.[112] Therefore, the cimasa of the polyptych, as well as two of the saints on the upper register, are yet to be identified; for that reason, the reconstruction of the polyptych is conjectural. Part of the problem is that not a single polyptych by Paolo survives intact. It is therefore unclear what the Santa Chiara Polyptych and the San Giacomo Maggiore Polyptych looked like originally. The Santa Chiara Polyptych was dismantled and reassembled a number of times, and its present frame is a combination of original and much later parts.[113] Its cimasa is missing, and it is unknown if it originally had a predella. The San Giacomo Maggiore Polyptych has a predella, but its original central compartment and cimasa are missing. What is evident from these two fragmentary polyptychs and

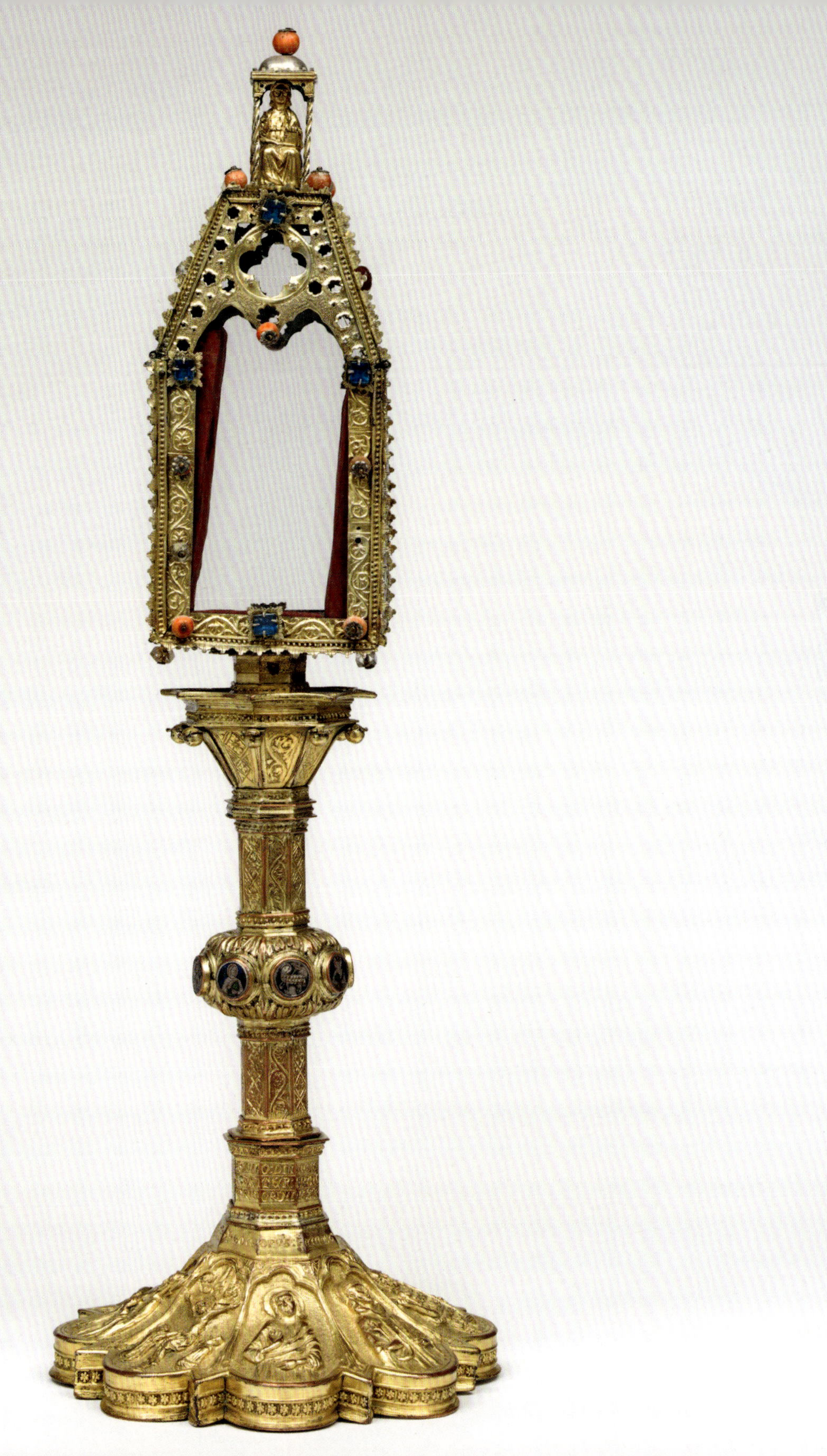

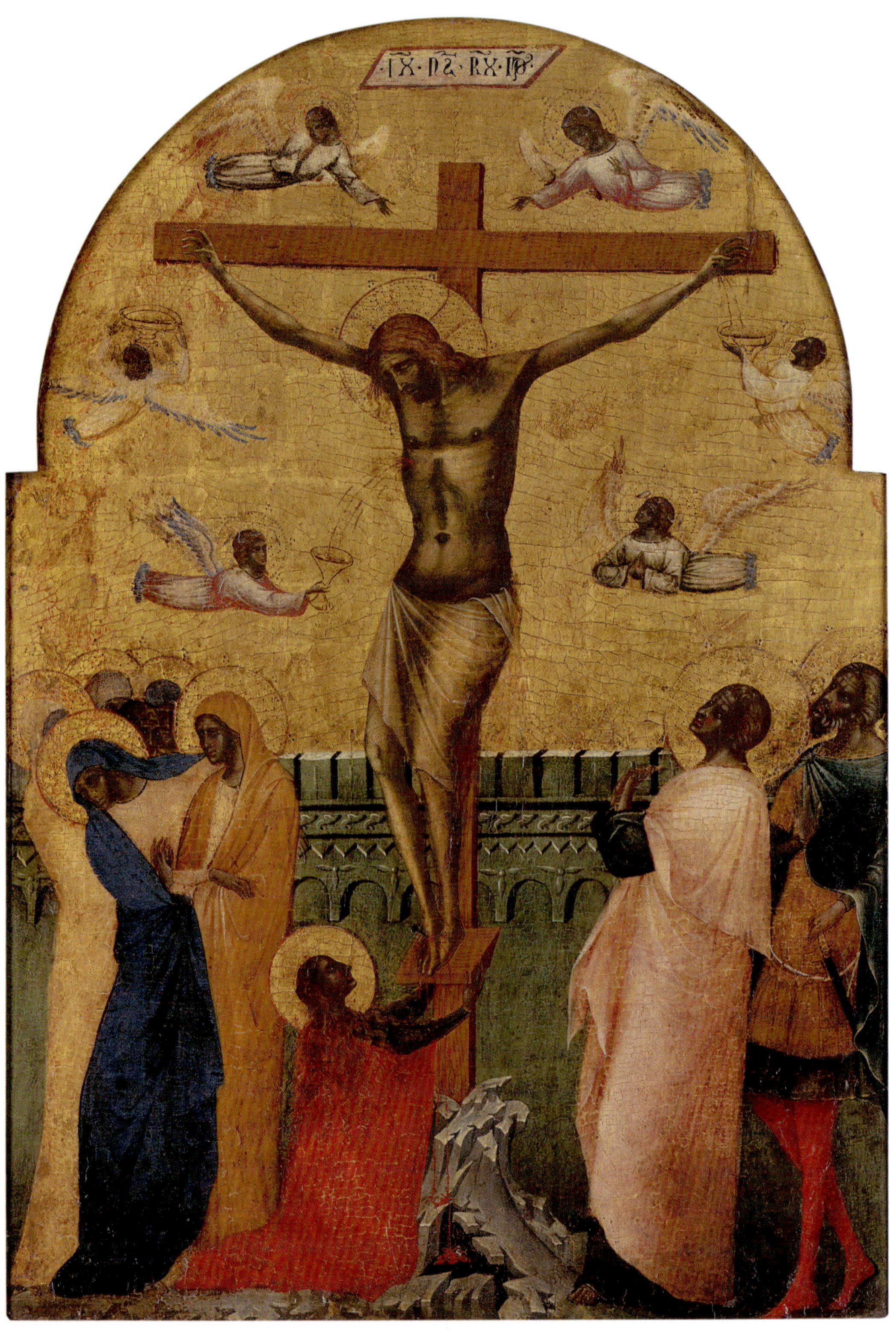

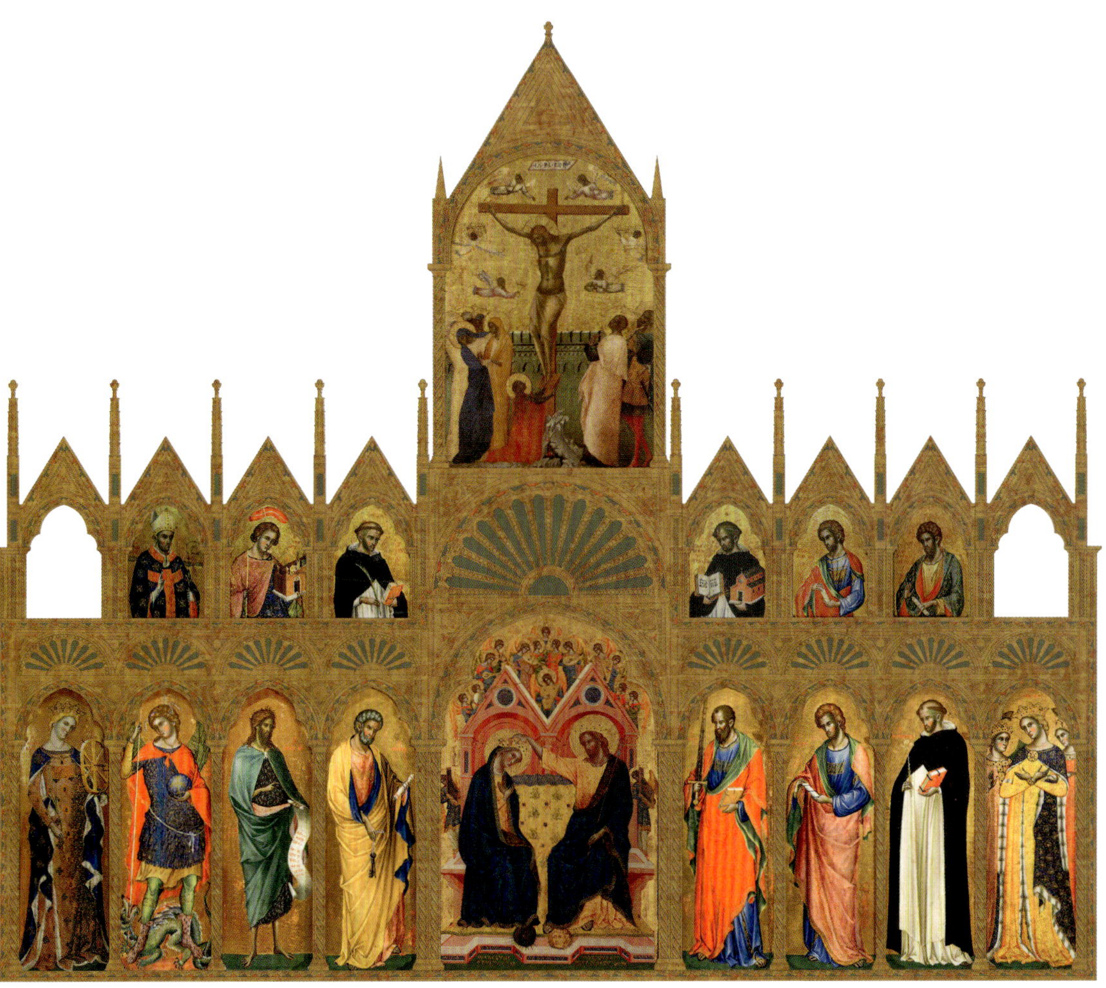

from a number of others by the workshop of Paolo, as well as other Venetian Trecento painters (such as Lorenzo Veneziano), is that the format of these altarpieces varied greatly. The most recent reconstruction of the polyptych, by John Witty, differs from Kiel's in a number of ways, most noticeably by the replacement of the shell-like structure above the *Coronation* with an acute arch, above which are three equally sized panels that would have formed the cimasa (fig. 33). The reconstruction is in great part inspired by the St. Lucy Polyptych in Krk, an altarpiece variously attributed to Paolo and his workshop.[114] It seems more likely, however, that the shell motif would have been retained by the carpenters responsible for Paolo's polyptych across the entire work. Moreover, no surviving work by Paolo presents an arch that is as acute as the one in the central panel of Witty's reconstruction. While the Frick panel has been cut at the top, it seems unlikely that anything would have been painted

Fig. 31
Paolo Veneziano
The Crucifixion, ca. 1350
Tempera on panel
38⅛ × 26⅝ in. (96.8 × 67.7 cm)
National Gallery of Victoria, Melbourne

Fig. 32
Reconstruction of Paolo and Giovanni Veneziano's *San Severino Polyptych* with the Melbourne *Crucifixion* as its cimasa

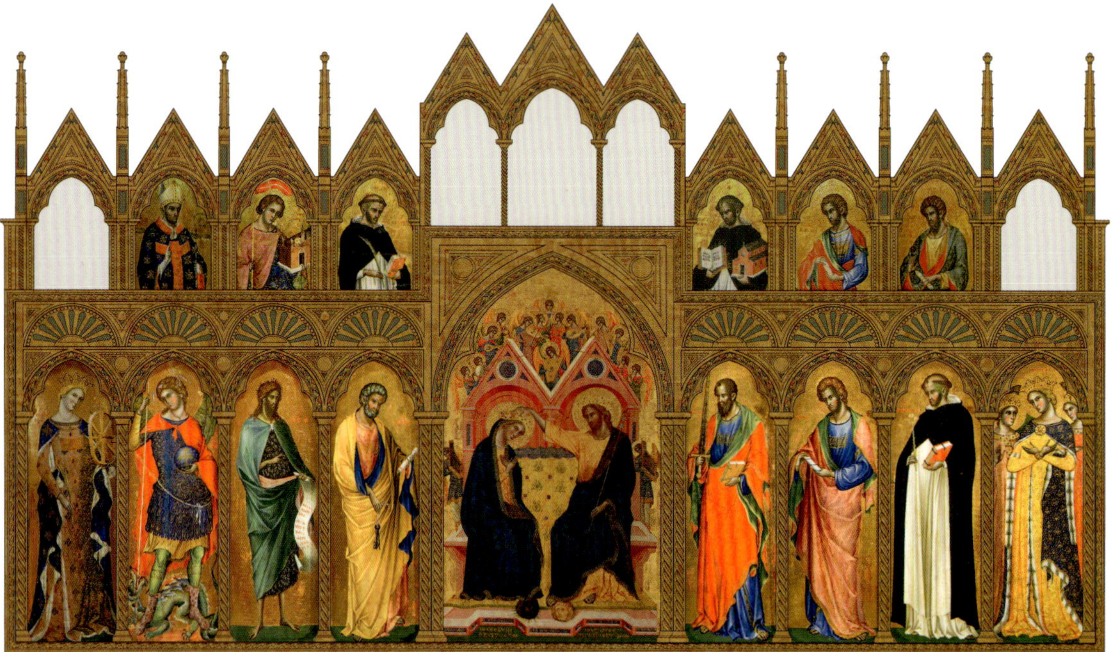

Fig. 33
John Witty's reconstruction of Paolo and Giovanni Veneziano's *San Severino Polyptych*, 2021

above the head of the topmost angel. The panel was therefore probably not much higher and was similar in shape to the central panel of the Santa Chiara Polyptych. While it remains to be established what formed its cimasa—and if it ever had a predella—the cimasa at the top was likely either a single panel or three panels of differing sizes, with the central one slightly larger than the middle one, as in other contemporary polyptychs by Venetian artists.[115]

The reconstruction (fig. 34) of the San Severino Polyptych remains hypothetical until new panels associated with it emerge. Another complication is that the physical evidence provided by the panels varies. While the San Severino *Fourteen Saints* retains the original thickness and structure of its support, the Frick's *Coronation* was considerably thinned and cradled before its acquisition by the Frick, making it impossible to gather any useful physical information from the back of the central panel. Reuniting the panels at some point, in New York or Italy, is desirable, especially in light of the different surviving parts of the San Severino Polyptych not having been together for at least two hundred years.

* * *

Paolo and Giovanni Veneziano's *Coronation of the Virgin* is a powerful exemplar of the beginnings of the Venetian tradition of painting. In the 1930s, Evelyn Sandberg Vavalà described the painting as the apex of Paolo Veneziano's art

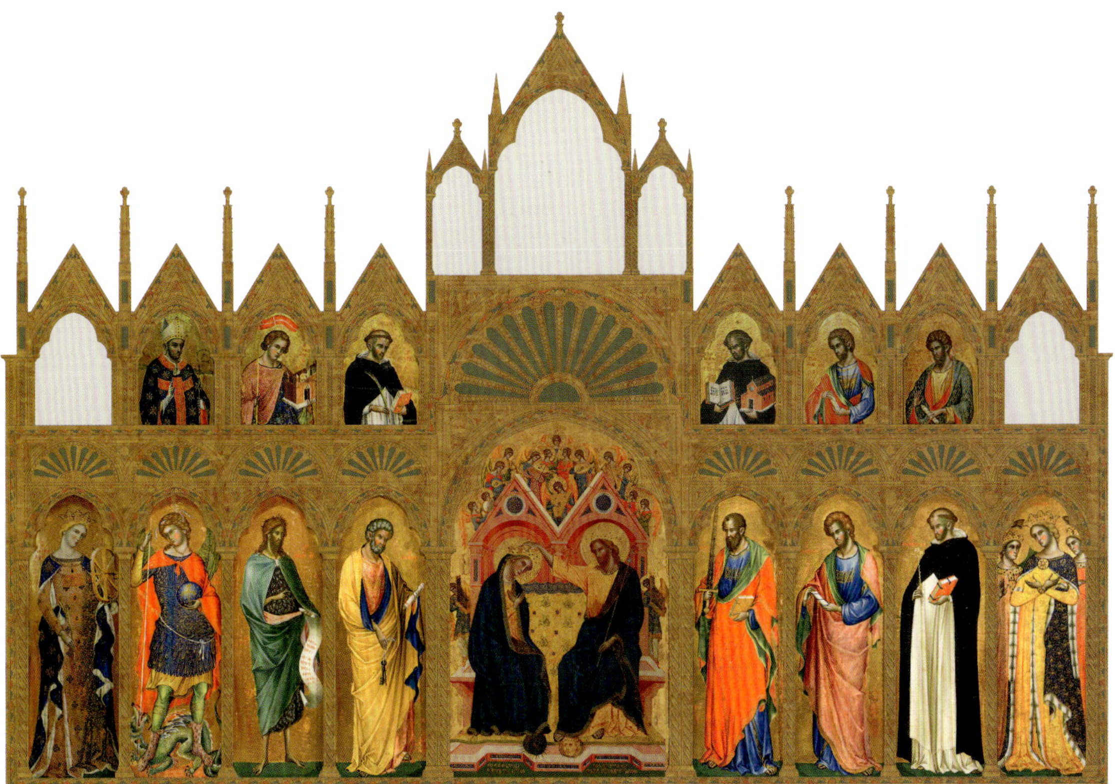

Fig. 34
Reconstruction of Paolo and Giovanni Veneziano's *San Severino Polyptych*

("il non plus ultra di Paolo Veneziano").[116] Roberto Longhi unforgettably praised the work of fourteenth-century painters in Venice, like Paolo, who were "extremely deferential to the value of the most luxurious materials that could be used, perfect technologists, aristocratic artisans who seem to work their paintings in tortoiseshell, lizard skin and gold."[117] Paolo's works, and his San Severino Polyptych, are examples of the stylistic hybridity of Venice at the time. As Michelangelo Muraro astutely commented:

> On the old block of the classical and Roman tradition, but perhaps more on the stupendous basis of the Byzantine technique and on a path toward the International Gothic (in which style all the city's architecture was then about to be renewed), the most diverse voices had been grafted: not only local and Italian, but, perhaps more decisively, the foreign and distant ones, spread among us by glassmakers, goldsmiths, illuminators who came from Burgundy and Germany, from Avignon, from Spain, etc.[118]

Venice and its art remain a unique and astonishing phenomenon in the European world, a place memorably described by the poet Petrarch, in his letters, as a "mundus alter"—another world.[119]

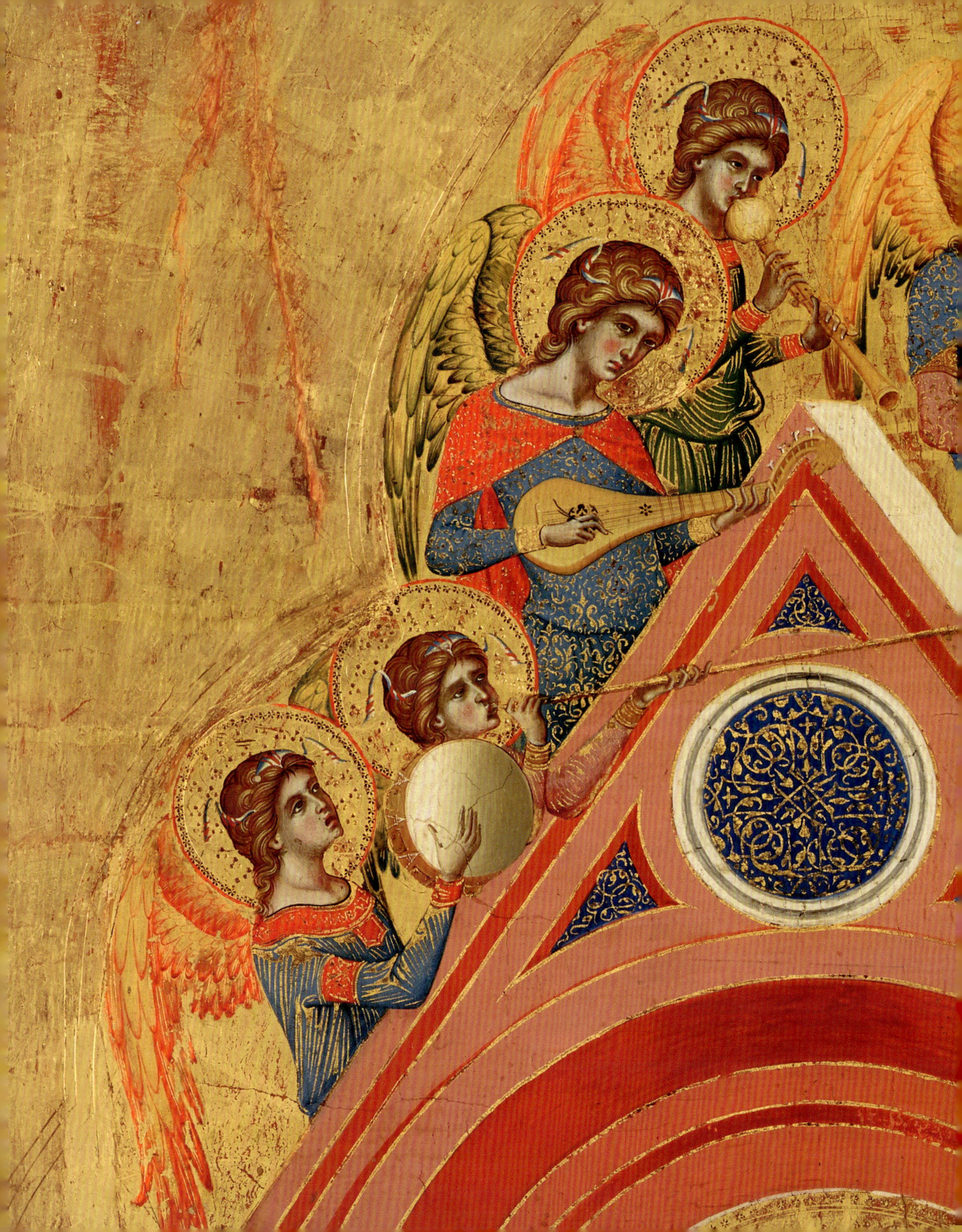

Notes

1 "Around the cushion, the word evokes the forgotten ones: Lorenzo Veneziano and Simone from Cusighe and Catarino and Iacobello and Master Paolo and Giambono and Semitecolo and Antonio and Andrea and Quirizio from Murano and the whole laborious family for whom the color, which was to become emulator of fire, was prepared in the ardent island of furnaces."

2 Norwich 1989, 203.

3 For Venice during Paolo Veneziano's lifetime, see Norwich 1989, 176–236; Ortalli 2002; L. Llewellyn and J. Witty in Los Angeles 2021, 1–5.

4 Norwich 1989, 268.

5 Ibid., 185–86.

6 Ibid., 191–97.

7 Ibid., 223–29.

8 Meiss 1951, 65.

9 Norwich 1989, 214–23.

10 Ibid., 235–36.

11 Meiss 1951.

12 Ibid., 70.

13 For the painting, see Muraro 1969, 153–55; Pedrocco 2003, 142–45, no. 2. The signature reads: + M.C.C.C.X.X.X.I.I.I. PAVLVS. D[E]. VENECIIS. PI[N]XIT. HOC. OPVS.

14 "il primo maestro a noi noto, quasi il fondatore—come è stato chiamato—della scuola pittorica veneziana"; Muraro 1969, 9.

15 For Paolo Veneziano, see, in particular, Cavalcaselle and Crowe 1887, 277–86; Testi 1909, 185–208; Van Marle 1924, 5–29; Sandberg Vavalà 1930; Fiocco 1930–31; Longhi 1946, 6–7, 44–46; Lasareff 1954; Moschini Marconi 1954; Pallucchini 1956; Pignatti 1961, 47–59; Pallucchini 1964, 17–60; Gamulin 1965; Levi D'Ancona 1965; Muraro 1969; Borla 1970; Gamulin 1970; Lucco 1986; Flores d'Arcais 1992, 24–42; Flores d'Arcais 1994, 250–66; Flores d'Arcais 1996; Gibbs 1996; Flores d'Arcais 2002; Pedrocco 2003; Boskovits 2009; Rullo 2014; Silver 2020; Los Angeles 2021.

16 For the lost painting, see Testi 1909, 192; Muraro 1969, 156; Pedrocco 2003, 142. The painting was apparently signed and dated: PAVLVS VENETVS FECIT HOC OPVS MCCCXXXIII.

17 As Sandberg Vavalà (1930, 160) accurately pointed out, "His birth cannot even remotely be estimated, as the various records are all in relation to payments and commissions, and fail to give us any personal information, such as the dates of his marriage or of the births of his sons."

18 For the Forzetta memorandum, see Avogadro degli Azzoni 1785, 150–52; Muraro 1969, 30–31, 86–87; Pedrocco 2003, 57–58; L. Llewellyn and J. Witty in Los Angeles 2021, 14–16.

19 "Et nota quod Mg. Marcus Pictor, qui moratur poenes locum Fratrum Minorum, fecit pannos theutonicos, qui sunt Tarvisii ad Sanctum Franciscum Minorum; qui panni sunt picti etiam Venetiis in loco Fr. Minorum et sunt ibi Fenestre vitree, facte manu dicti Magistri et bene facte. Nam quidam Frater Theutonicus fecit omnia ab antiquo Tarvisium; et nota quod supradictus Mag. Marcus Pictor qui moratur penes Sanctam Mariam Fratrum Minorum de Venetiis habet unum Fratrem nomine Paulum Pictorem, qui moratur poenes dictam Sanctam mariam Fr. Minorum: qui habet in carta designatam mortem Sancti Francisci et Virginis gloriose, sicut picte sunt ad modo Theutonicum in panno ad locum Min. in Tarvisio"; Muraro 1969, 86–87.

20 "Magister Paulus pictor filius quondam Martini pictoris de contrata Sancti Luche de Veneciis . . ."; Pedrocco 2003, 54.

21 For Martino and Marco, see Muraro 1969, 29–32; Borla 1970; Zuliani 1989; Pedrocco 2003, 54–59; Guarnieri 2006, 38.

22 For the two triptychs, see Muraro 1969, 117, 131, 158; Pedrocco 2003, 70, 126, 131, 146–49, 154–55, nos. 5, 6, 8; L. Llewellyn in Los Angeles 2021, 102–19, nos. 3–6. For Paolo Veneziano's triptychs for personal devotion, see L. Llewellyn in Los Angeles 2021, 25–47.

23 For the Santa Chiara Polyptych, see Muraro 1969, 69–70, 147–48; Pedrocco 2003, 61, 150–53, no. 7. The polyptych is dated to the mid-1330s in Van Marle 1924, 7; Pedrocco 2003, 61, 150–53, no. 7; Boskovitz 2009, 87n.13; and to the early 1350s in Pallucchini 1964, 46; Muraro 1969, 69–70, 147–48; Flores d'Arcais 1992, 40; Silver 2020, 73. Based on stylistic analysis, the views of De Marchi (1995, 243n.13), who dates the polyptych between 1333 and 1345, and of Pedrocco (2003, 61, 150–53, no. 7), who narrows the date between 1333 and 1336, seem the most likely conclusion.

24 Muraro 1969, 40–42, 145–46; Pedrocco 2003, 80, 83, 164–65, no. 13; Guarnieri 2015.

25 Muraro 1969, 46, 123; Pedrocco 2003, 76, 80, 166–67, no. 14. The painting is signed: PA[VULVS] MCCCXL M[ENS]E AG[VSTI] / HA[NC] PI[NXIT].

26 EGO PAULUS PICTOR SANCTI LUCE TT.SS.; Muraro 1969, 87.
27 Muraro 1969, 87. Other scholars, however, believe that this Paolo may be another artist, possibly a carpenter; see Pedrocco 2003, 86.
28 "Le commissioni per le tombe ducali e per le feste pubbliche, la presenza dell'artista in Palazzo Ducale e nella Basilica Marciana, costituiscono a mio avviso le tappe fondamentali della linea di sviluppo dell'arte di Maestro Paolo"; Muraro 1969, 17. For Paolo as the official painter of the Republic, see Muraro 1969, 40–57; Pedrocco 2003, 86–92.
29 For the reign of Andrea Dandolo and its culture, see Muraro 1969, 51–52; Muraro 1974; Ravegnani 1986; Belting 2006.
30 For the Pala d'Oro, see Hahnloser and Polacco 1994.
31 For the Pala Feriale, see Di Carpegna 1951; Muraro 1969, 53–56, 143; Goffen 1996; Fiocco 1994; Pedrocco 2003, 86–92, 170–73, no. 16.
32 The first scene to the left in the lower tier, representing St. Peter Consecrating St. Mark as Bishop of Alexandria, includes the date M.C.C.C.XLV. M[ENSI]S. AP[RI]LIS. DIE. XXII. The fifth scene from the left, also on the lower tier, representing St. Mark Saving the Ship Carrying His Relics to Venice, includes the signature MAG[ISTE] R. PAVLVS. CV[M]. LVCA ET. IOH[ANN]E. FILIIS. SVIS. PINXERV[N]T. / HOC. OPVS. For the practical functioning of the Pala Feriale, see Guarnieri 2019.
33 Interestingly, Paolo and Caterina named three of their sons after three of the four evangelists (Mark, Luke, and John).
34 "Die 20 mensi ianuarii dedimus ducatos 20 auri magistro Paulo pentore sancti luce pro pintura unius anchone facte in ecclesia sancti Nicolai de Palacio"; Muraro 1969, 88.
35 For the paintings, see Muraro 1969, 42, 116–17; Pedrocco 2003, 92, 174–75, no. 17; L. Llewellyn in Los Angeles 2021, 124–27, no. 9. The Florence paintings were first connected to the Doge's Palace commission by Pallucchini (1964, 39–40).
36 + PAVLVS DE. VENECIIS. PI[N]XIT / M.C.C.C.XLVII. For the painting, see Muraro 1969, 58–59, 110–11; Pedrocco 2003, 176–77, no. 18.
37 "formicolìo ornamentale"; Longhi 1946, 45.
38 Muraro 1969, 88.
39 For the crucifix, see Gamulin 1965; Muraro 1969, 116; Pedrocco 2003, 178–79, no. 19; Pilo 2005; Guarnieri 2010, 135–40.
40 Pedrocco 2003, 178.
41 Muraro 1969, 88; Pedrocco 2003, 178.
42 This was first suggested by Muraro (1969, 66, 70).
43 Muraro 1969, 58–71.
44 "Un'immobilità ieratica e superstiziosa si è ormai decisamente sostituita alla preziosità dei colori e alla grazia luminosa che l'artista aveva sempre amato. Si irrigidiscono gli schemi e le forme: le decorazioni diventano grosse e opache; i profili sono ridotti a larve; l'esecuzione pittorica è sempre più frettolosa e trascurata"; Muraro 1969, 67.
45 For Paolo's work along the Adriatic coast, see, especially, Rimini 2002; Baradel and Guarnieri 2019.
46 For the serial production of some of these works, see Guarnieri 2010; L. Llewellyn in Los Angeles 2021, 25–47.
47 For the best general outlook on Venetian altarpieces in the Trecento and the thriving market for them, see Silver 2020.
48 For the Chioggia polyptych, see Muraro 1969, 59–60, 62–64, 112–13; Pedrocco 2003, 180–83, no. 20.
49 For the so-called Campana polyptych in Paris, see Muraro 1969, 129–30; Pedrocco 2003, 105–6, 194–95, no. 25.
50 For the Piran polyptych, see Muraro 1969, 133; L. Morozzi in Rimini 2002, 158–61, no. 28; Pedrocco 2003, 105–6, 196–97, no. 26; Guarnieri 2019, 45–49.
51 The altarpiece has been dated between the mid-1340s and the 1350s. Stylistically, I believe it to date from the 1350s. For the polyptych, see Muraro 1969, 62, 107–8; De Marchi 1995, 241; Pedrocco 2003, 97–98, 184–87, no. 21; Guarnieri 2005, 57; Minardi 2012, 320; Silver 2020, 71.
52 Muraro 1969, 89.
53 For Marco, see De Marchi 1995.
54 Gibbs 1996, 29.
55 Muraro 1969, 89.
56 For the painting, see *Sitzungsberichte* 1868, 37–41; Munich 1869, 31, no. 12; Sigmaringen 1875, 246–47; Von Lehner 1883, 75, no. 221; Cavalcaselle and Crowe 1887, 285–86; Harck 1893, 388–89; Testi 1909, 196–98; Rieffel 1924, 57; Van Marle 1924, 6–7, 12–14; Sandberg Vavalà 1930, 160, 166, 177, no. 18; Bettini 1940, 101; Pallucchini 1950, 8; Lasareff 1954, 88; Pignatti 1961, 59; Pallucchini 1964, 52; *Frick Collection* 1968, 266–71; Muraro 1969, 71–72, 74–75, 127–28; Lucco 1986, 182; Flores d'Arcais 1992, 25, 40, 42; Flores d'Arcais 1994, 262–64; Flores d'Arcais 1996,

23–24; Gibbs 1996, 33; Pedrocco 2003, 123, 126, 204, no. 30; Guarnieri 2006, 35; De Marchi 2014, 16–19; J. Witty in Los Angeles 2021, 100–101, no. 2.

57 For the fabric in Paolo's painting, see Klesse 1967, 270, 370; J. Witty in Los Angeles 2021, 64–67.

58 For the identification of the instruments, see *Frick Collection* 1968, 270.

59 Meiss 1951, 153–55.

60 Ibid., 43–44.

61 For the Master of the Washington Coronation, see Muraro 1969, 29–30; Zuliani 1989; Pedrocco 2003, 58–59; Guarnieri 2006, 38. The most lucid reading of the identity and career of the Master is Guarnieri 2007.

62 For the fragment, see Muraro 1969, 134; Pedrocco 2003, 198–99, no. 27.

63 For the textiles, see King 1965; Muraro 1969, 120; Baradel 2019.

64 King 1965, 18.

65 For Guariento, see, most recently, Padua 2011.

66 Helen Clay Frick Papers, Series XI: Travel—Volumes—Italy, 1925—Vol. 3, 28. The Frick Collection/Frick Art Reference Library Archives.

67 For Lorenzo Veneziano, see Guarnieri 2006.

68 Helen Clay Frick Papers. Series V: Art Files—Volumes—Italian Art—Venetian Painting. The Frick Collection/Frick Art Reference Library Archives.

69 A copy of the booklet is preserved in The Frick Collection/Frick Art Reference Library Archives.

70 All of the correspondence about the painting's acquisition is preserved in The Frick Collection—Board of Trustees Files, 1920–31—Acquisitions—Veneziano "Coronation of the Virgin." The Frick Collection/Frick Art Reference Library Archives.

71 For the collecting of Paolo Veneziano in the United States, see L. Llewellyn and J. Witty in Los Angeles 2021, 19–20.

72 The Getty Research Institute. Knoedler Stock Book 8, stock no. A511, page 68, row 3.

73 "Hr. J. Maillinger eröffnete die Sitzung mit einem Vortrage über ein in seinem Besitze befindliches Gemälde des Meisters Paolo Veneziano mit der Jahreszahl 1358"; *Sitzungsberichte* 1868, 37.

74 Munich 1869, 31, no. 12.

75 Cavalcaselle and Crowe 1887, 285–86.

76 "die Herkunft des Bildes, welches aus einer jetzt als Kohlenmagazin benutzten Capelle in der Nähe von Ravenna stammt"; *Sitzungsberichte* 1868, 38.

77 "später bem Grafen Baccinetti Gehörte"; Sigmaringen 1875, 246. "appartenuto a un conte Baccinetti"; Harck 1893, 388.

78 The family surname, Bacinetti, is also often spelled as Baccinetti.

79 For the two palaces, see Graziani and Adversi Selvi 2009, 301n.1. The palazzo decorated by Giani on Via SS. Giovanni e Paolo (now Via d'Azeglio) was the grander of the two buildings; the other was on Strada degli Strigoni (now Via C. Cattaneo).

80 For Marianna Bacinetti, see Plebe 1963; Graziani and Adversi Selvi 2009.

81 A small part of Marianna's archive remains in private hands; see Squadroni 1981. It has been impossible to consult these papers while preparing this book.

82 Graziani and Adversi Selvi 2009, 301n.1.

83 Von Lehner 1883, 75, no. 221; Harck 1893, 388.

84 "Il quadro più rilevante del trecento, in codesto Museo"; Harck 1893, 388.

85 For the collection and its history, see Harck 1893.

86 "La collezione Sigmaringen è circa un museo Poldi-Pezzoli, tedesco"; Harck 1893, 387.

87 *Frick Collection* 1968, 270.

88 In the copy of the collection's catalogue (Von Lehner 1883) preserved in the castle at Sigmaringen, the entry for Paolo Veneziano's painting (75, no. 221) is annotated "sold 1928" (*verkauft 1928*).

89 B. Davidson in *Frick Collection* 1968, 268.

90 Helen Clay Frick Papers, Series XI: Travel—Volumes—Italy, 1925—Vol. 3. The Frick Collection/Frick Art Reference Library Archives.

91 Sandberg Vavalà 1930, 165, 171–72, 177, no. 3. In fact, Berenson (1905, 360) had already suggested the idea of the painting being by Paolo Veneziano and his workshop.

92 "Che il complesso di figure del polittico sanseverinate . . . si avvicini all''Incoronazione' Frick non mi pare dubbio"; Pallucchini 1950, 8.

93 Kiel 1977.

94 For the panels, see Ranaldi 1820, 88–89; Servanzi Collio 1838; Valentini 1868, 123–24; Aleandri 1897, 136; Berenson 1905, 360; Testi 1909, 229; Van Marle 1924, 43; Sandberg Vavalà 1930, 165–71; Pallucchini 1950, 8–10, 13–16; Lasareff 1954, 89; Pallucchini 1964, 51–53; Muraro 1969, 70–71, 135–36; Kiel 1977; Gibbs 1996, 33; Marchi 2000, 35–38; A. Marchi in Rimini 2002, 166–67, no. 31; Pedrocco 2003, 202–3, no. 29; Guarnieri 2006, 22, 35, 82, 203; Minardi

2012, 316–32; De Marchi 2014, 16–18; Paciaroni 2018; J. Witty in Los Angeles 2021, 98–99, no. 1.

95 Ranaldi 1820; later published in Ranaldi 1837, XXX–XXXI; Paciaroni 2018, 10–11.

96 Paciaroni 2018, 12.

97 Servanzi Collio 1838; Paciaroni 2018, 15.

98 "non è assolutamente di Allegretto, ma di altra scuola. La crede di scuola veneta antica"; Paciaroni 2018, 15.

99 "è sparita, né si sa chi l'abbia involata." Valentini 1868, 178n.2; Paciaroni 2018, 16.

100 Paciaroni 2018, 17–18.

101 Aleandri 1896, 4; Aleandri 1897, 136; Paciaroni 2018, 25.

102 For the decoration of Dominican churches in the thirteenth and fourteenth centuries, see Cannon 2013.

103 Kiel 1977.

104 For the history of the church, see Paciaroni 2018, 32–34.

105 While acknowledging the origin of the San Severino panels, Paciaroni (2018) is the only one to openly reject Kiel's proposal that the Frick's *Coronation* was at the center of the polyptych. His arguments, however, are not convincing.

106 For a precise analysis of the gilding in this work, see De Marchi 2014, 16–19.

107 Paciaroni 2018, 35–42.

108 Ibid., 36–37.

109 For the reliquary, see, most recently, J. Witty in Los Angeles 2021, 130–31, no. 11.

110 Marchi 2000; Paciaroni 2018, 54–60.

111 Marchi 2000, 38; A. Marchi in Rimini 2002, 166.

112 J. Witty (in Los Angeles 2021, 94), for example, rejects the proposal.

113 I would like to thank Valeria Poletto and Roberto Saccuman for a number of discussions in front of the polyptych while it was being restored under the auspices of Save Venice.

114 J. Witty in Los Angeles 2021, 95–97.

115 I would like to thank Roberto Saccuman for a number of discussions relating to the virtual reconstruction of the San Severino Polyptych.

116 Muraro 1969, 100, 127.

117 "Deferentissimi al pregio delle più lussuose materie adoperabili, tecnologi perfetti, artigiani aristocratici che sembrano lavorare i loro dipinti in tartaruga, pelle di ramarro e oro"; Longhi 1946, 6.

118 "Sul vecchio ceppo della tradizione classica e romana, ma forse piú sulla stupenda base della tecnica bizantina e sulla via del gotico-fiorito (che del resto ormai stava per rinnovare tutte le architetture della città) si erano innestate le voci piú diverse: non solo locali e italiane, ma, forse piú determinanti, quelle straniere e lontane, diffuse fra noi da vetrai, dagli orefici, dai miniatori che provenivano dalla Borgogna e dalla Germania, da Avignone, dalla Spagna, ecc."; Muraro 1969, 74.

119 Muraro 1974, 166.

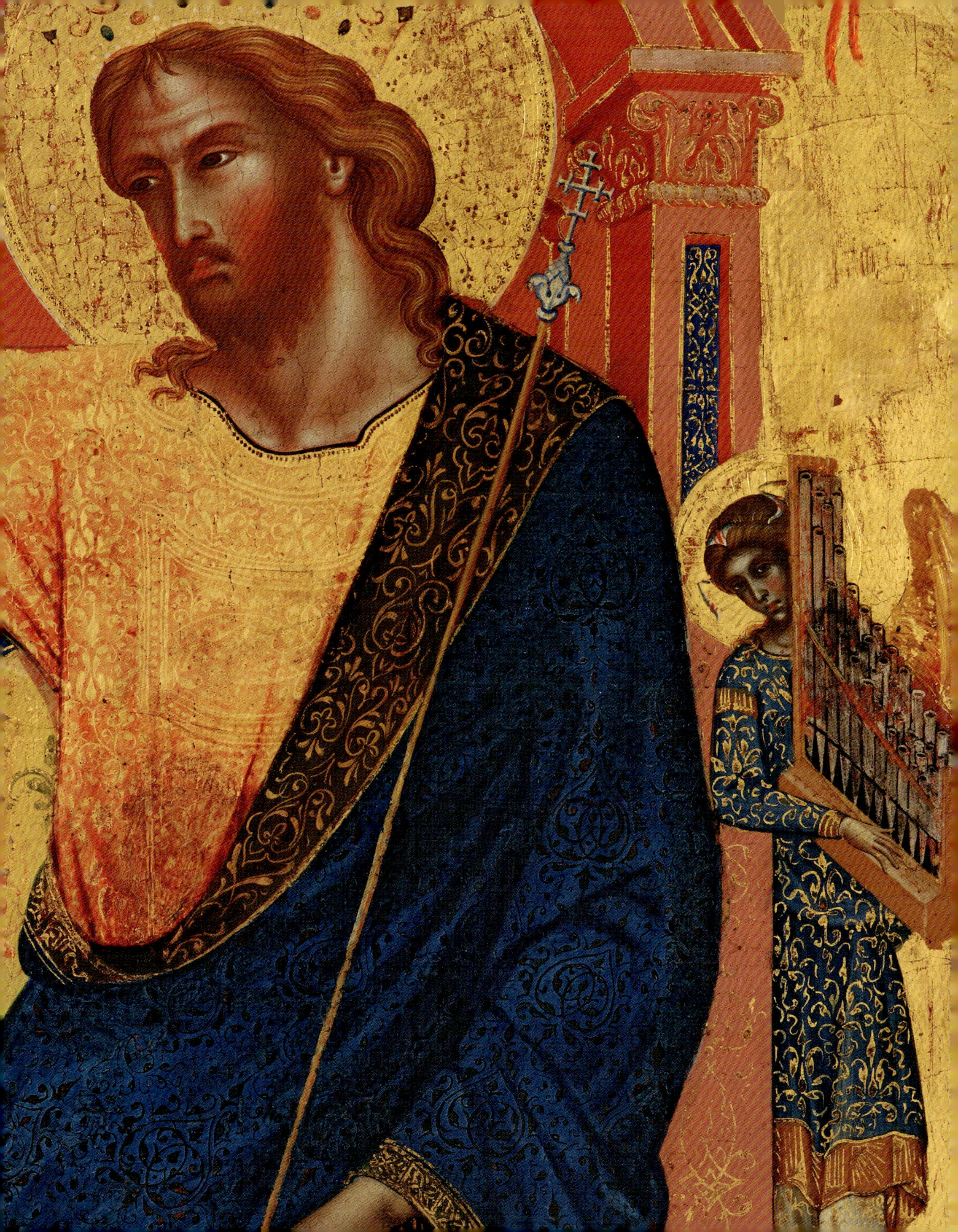

BIBLIOGRAPHY

Aleandri 1896 Aleandri, Vittorio Emanuele. "Gli oggetti d'arte esistenti nella Civica Pinacoteca di Sanseverino-Marche." *Arte e Storia* 5 (1896): 99–101.

Aleandri 1897 Aleandri, Vittorio Emanuele. "La Pinacoteca di Sanseverino Marche." *Le Gallerie Nazionali Italiane. Notizie e Documenti* 3 (1897): 136–37.

Avogadro degli Azzoni 1785 Avogadro degli Azzoni, Rambaldo. "Trattato della zecca e delle monete che ebbero corso in Trevigi, fin tutto il secolo XIV." In *Monete e zecche d'Italia*, vol. 4, edited by Guido Antonio Zanetti. Bologna, 1785.

Baradel 2019 Baradel, Valentina. "Diramazioni adriatiche di botteghe veneziane. L'isola di Veglia (Krk), da Paolo Veneziano a Jacobello del Fiore." In Baradel and Guarnieri 2019, 57–75.

Baradel and Guarnieri 2019 Baradel, Valentina, and Cristina Guarnieri. *La Serenissima via mare: Arte e cultura tra Venezia e il Quarnaro*. Padua, 2019.

Belting 2002 Belting, Hans. "Bisanzio a Venezia non è Bisanzio a Bisanzio." In Rimini 2002, 71–79.

Belting 2006 Belting, Hans. "Dandolo's Dreams: Venetian State Art and Byzantium." In *Byzantium: Faith and Power (1261–1557): Perspectives on Late Byzantine Art and Culture*, edited by Sarah T. Brooks, 138–53. New Haven and London, 2006.

Berenson 1905 Berenson, Bernard. *The Venetian Painters of the Renaissance with an Index of Their Works*. New York, 1905.

Bettini 1940 Bettini, Sergio. *Pitture cretesi-veneziane, slave e italiane del Museo Nazionale di Ravenna*. Ravenna, 1940.

Borla 1970 Borla, Silvino. "Paolo Veneziano e il fratello Marco." *Arte Veneta* 24 (1970): 199–204.

Boskovits 2009 Boskovits, Miklós. "Paolo Veneziano: riflessioni sul percorso." *Arte Cristiana* 97 (2009): 81–90, 161–70.

Cannon 2013 Cannon, Joanna. *Religious Poverty, Visual Riches: Art in the Dominican Churches of Central Italy in the Thirteenth and Fourteenth Centuries*. New Haven and London, 2013.

Cavalcaselle and Crowe 1887 Cavalcaselle, Giovanni Battista, and Joseph Arthur Crowe. *Storia della pittura in Italia dal secolo II al secolo XVI*. Vol. 4. Florence, 1887.

De Marchi 1995 De Marchi, Andrea. "Una tavola nella Narodna Galeria di Ljubljana e una proposta per Marco di Paolo Veneziano." In *Gotika v Sloveniji: Nastajanje kulturnega prostora med Alpami, Panonijo in Jadranom*, edited by Janez Hoefler, 241–56. Ljubljana, 1995.

De Marchi 2014 De Marchi, Andrea. "La ricezione dell'oro: una chiave di lettura per la storia della pittura veneziana dal Duecento al Tardogotico." *Arte Veneta* 71 (2014): 9–32.

Di Carpegna 1951 Di Carpegna, Nolfo. "La 'coperta' della Pala d'Oro di Paolo Veneziano." *Bollettino d'Arte* 36 (1951): 55–66.

Fiocco 1930–31 Fiocco, Giuseppe. "Primizie di Maestro Paolo Veneziano." *Dedalo* 11 (1930–31): 877–94.

Fiocco 1994 Fiocco, Giuseppe. "La Pala Feriale di Maestro Paolo Veneziano." In *La Pala d'Oro*, edited by Hans Robert Hahnloser and Renato Polacco, 163–67. Venice, 1994.

Flores d'Arcais 1992 Flores d'Arcais, Francesca. "Venezia." In *La pittura nel Veneto: Il Trecento*, edited by Mauro Lucco, 17–42. Milan, 1992.

Flores d'Arcais 1994 Flores d'Arcais, Francesca. "La pittura." In *Storia di Venezia: Temi. L'arte*, edited by Rodolfo Pallucchini, 237–303. Rome, 1994.

Flores d'Arcais 1996 Flores d'Arcais, Francesca. "Tradizione e innovazione nella pittura veneziana del Trecento: Paolo e intorno a Paolo." *Hortus Artium Medievalium* 2 (1996): 19–25.

Flores d'Arcais 2002 Flores d'Arcais, Francesca. "Paolo Veneziano e la pittura del Trecento in Adriatico." In Rimini 2002, 19–31.

***Frick Collection* 1968** *The Frick Collection: An Illustrated Catalogue.* Vol. 2, *Paintings: French, Italian and Spanish*. New York, 1968.

Gamulin 1965 Gamulin, Grgo. "Un crocifisso di Maestro Paolo ed altri due del Trecento." *Arte Veneta* 19 (1965): 32–43.

Gamulin 1970 Gamulin, Grgo. "Di un libro su Paolo da Venezia." *Arte Veneta* 24 (1970): 255–67.

Gibbs 1996 Gibbs, Robert. "Paolo Veneziano." In *Dictionary of Art*, vol. 24, edited by Jane Turner, 29–34. Oxford and New York, 1996.

Goffen 1996 Goffen, Rona. "Il paliotto della Pala d'Oro di Paolo Veneziano e la committenza del doge Andrea Dandolo." In *San Marco: Aspetti storici e agiografici. Atti del Convegno internazionale di studi, Venezia, 26–29 aprile 1994*, edited by Antonio Niero, 313–33. Venice, 1996.

Graziani and Adversi Selvi 2009 Graziani, Natale, and Maria Luisa Adversi Selvi. *Amante reale: La Marchesa Florenzi e il re di Bavaria*. Milan, 2009.

Guarnieri 2005 Guarnieri, Cristina. "Le polyptyque pour l'église San Giacomo Maggiore de Bologne dans l'œuvre de Lorenzo Veneziano." In *Autour de Lorenzo Veneziano: Fragments de polyptyques vénitiens du XIV siècle*, edited by Michel Laclotte, 57–81. Exh. cat. Tours (Musée des Beaux-Arts). Milan, 2005.

Guarnieri 2006 Guarnieri, Cristina. *Lorenzo Veneziano*. Milan, 2006.

Guarnieri 2007 Guarnieri, Cristina. "Il passaggio tra due generazioni: dal Maestro dell'Incoronazione a Paolo Veneziano." In *Il secolo di Giotto nel Veneto*, edited by Giovanna Valenzano and Federica Toniolo, 153–77. Venice, 2007.

Guarnieri 2010 Guarnieri, Cristina. "Per la restituzione di due croci perdute di Paolo Veneziano: il leone marciano del Museo Correr e i dolenti della Galleria Sabauda." In *Medioevo adriatico: Circolazione di modelli, opere, maestri*, edited by Federica Toniolo and Giovanna Valenzano, 134–46. Rome, 2010.

Guarnieri 2015 Guarnieri, Cristina. "Il monumento funebre di Francesco Dandolo nella Sala del Capitolo ai Frari." In *Santa Maria Gloriosa dei Frari: Immagini di devozione, spazi della fede*, edited by Carlo Corsato and Deborah Howard, 151–62. Padua, 2015.

Guarnieri 2019 Guarnieri, Cristina. "Lo svelamento rituale delle reliquie e le pale ribaltabili di Paolo Veneziano sulla costa istriano-dalmata." In Baradel and Guarnieri 2019, 39–53.

Hahnloser and Polacco 1994 Hahnloser, Hans Robert, and Renato Polacco, eds. *La Pala d'Oro*. Venice, 1994.

Harck 1893 Harck, Fritz. "Quadri italiani nelle gallerie private di Germania." *Archivio Storico dell'Arte* 6 (1893): 387–90.

Kiel 1977 Kiel, Hanna. "Das Polyptychon von Paolo und Giovanni Veneziano in Sanseverino Marche." *Pantheon* 35 (1977): 105–8.

King 1965 King, Donald. "A Venetian Embroidered Altar Frontal." *Victoria and Albert Museum Bulletin* 1 (1965): 15–25.

Klesse 1967 Klesse, Brigitte. *Seidenstoffe in der italianischen Malerei des 14. Jahrhunderts*. Bern, 1967.

Lasareff 1954 Lasareff, Victor. "Maestro Paolo e la pittura veneziana del suo tempo." *Arte Veneta* 8 (1954): 77–89.

Levi D'Ancona 1965 Levi D'Ancona, Mirella. "La Mariegola della Scuola Grande di S. Marco al Museo Correr." *Bollettino dei Musei Civici Veneziani* 10 (1965): 2–20.

Longhi 1946 Longhi, Roberto. *Viatico per cinque secoli di pittura veneziana*. Florence, 1946.

Los Angeles 2021 Laura Llewellyn and John Witty, eds. *Paolo Veneziano: The Art of Painting in 14th-Century Venice*. Exh. cat. Los Angeles (J. Paul Getty Museum). New York and London, 2021.

Lucco 1986 Lucco, Mauro. "Pittura del Trecento a Venezia." In *La Pittura in Italia: Il Duecento e il Trecento*, vol. 1, 176–88. Milan, 1986.

Marchi 2000 Marchi, Alessandro. "Trecento veneziano nelle terre adriatiche marchigiane." In *Pittura veneta nelle Marche*, edited by Valter Curzi, 29–51. Milan, 2000.

Meiss 1951 Meiss, Millard. *Painting in Florence and Siena after the Black Death: The Arts, Religion, and Society in the Mid-Fourteenth Century*. Princeton, 1951.

Minardi 2012 Minardi, Mauro. "Studi sulla collezione Nevin: i dipinti veneti del XIV e XV secolo." *Saggi e Memorie di Storia dell'Arte* 12 (2012): 315–50.

Moschini Marconi 1954 Moschini Marconi, Sandra. "Un'altra Madonna di Paolo Veneziano." *Arte Veneta* 8 (1954): 90–92.

Munich 1869 *Katalog der Ausstellung von Gemälden älterer Meister*. Exh. cat. Munich (Kunstausstellungsgebäude gegenüber der Glyptothek), 1869.

Muraro 1969 Muraro, Michelangelo. *Paolo da Venezia*. Milan, 1969.

Muraro 1974 Muraro, Michelangelo. "Petrarca, Paolo Veneziano e la cultura artistica alla corte del doge Andrea Dandolo." In *Petrarca, Venezia e il Veneto*, edited by Giorgio Padoan, 157–68. Florence, 1974.

Norwich 1989 Norwich, John Julius. *A History of Venice*. New York, 1989.

Ortalli 2002 Ortalli, Gherardo. "La Venezia di Paolo Veneziano: tra mare, terra e laguna." In Rimini 2002, 45–55.

Paciaroni 2018 Paciaroni, Raoul. *Il polittico sanseverinate di Paolo Veneziano*. San Severino Marche, 2018.

Padua 2011 Davide Banzato, Francesca Flores d'Arcais, and Anna Maria Spiazzi, eds. *Guariento*. Exh. cat. Padua (Palazzo del Monte di Pietà). Venice, 2011.

Pallucchini 1950 Pallucchini, Rodolfo. "Commento alla mostra di Ancona." *Arte Veneta* 4 (1950): 7–32.

Pallucchini 1956 Pallucchini, Rodolfo. "Nota per Paolo Veneziano." In *Scritti di storia dell'arte in onore di Lionello Venturi*, 121–37. Rome, 1956.

Pallucchini 1964 Pallucchini, Rodolfo. *La pittura veneziana del Trecento*. Venice and Rome, 1964.

Pedrocco 2003 Pedrocco, Filippo. *Paolo Veneziano*. Venice, 2003.

Pignatti 1961 Pignatti, Terisio. *Origini della pittura veneziana*. Bergamo, 1961.

Pilo 2005 Pilo, Giuseppe Maria. "La *Crux de Media Ecclesia* di Paolo Veneziano nella chiesa dei Domenicani a Ragusa: un capolavoro del Trecento italiano risarcito." In *Gli affanni del collezionista: Studi di storia dell'arte in memoria di Feliciano Benvenuti*, edited by Chiara Callegari, 21–25. Padua, 2005.

Plebe 1963 Plebe, Armando. "Bacinetti Florenzi-Waddington, Marianna." In *Dizionario Biografico degli Italiani*, vol. 5, 58–59. Rome, 1963.

Ranaldi 1820 Ranaldi, Giuseppe. *Memorie di belle arti*. Vol. 2, Ms. n. 31, 1820. Biblioteca Comunale, San Severino Marche.

Ranaldi 1837 Ranaldi, Giuseppe. *Memorie storiche di S. Maria del Glorioso presso la città di Sanseverino nel Piceno*. Macerata, 1837.

Ravegnani 1986 Ravegnani, Giorgio. "Dandolo, Andrea." In *Dizionario Biografico degli Italiani*, vol. 32, 432–38. Rome, 1986.

Rieffel 1924 Rieffel, Franz. "Das Fürstlich Hohenzollernsche Museum zu Sigmaringen: Gemälde und Bildwerke." *Städel-Jahrbuch* 3–4 (1924): 55–74.

Rimini 2002 Francesca Flores d'Arcais and Giovanni Gentili, eds. *Il Trecento adriatico: Paolo Veneziano e la pittura tra Oriente e Occidente*. Exh. cat. Rimini (Castel Sismondo), 2002.

Rullo 2014 Rullo, Alessandra. "Veneziano, Paolo." In *Dizionario Biografio degli Italiani*, vol. 81, 190–94. Rome, 2014.

Sandberg Vavalà 1930 Sandberg Vavalà, Evelyn. "Maestro Paolo Veneziano." *Burlington Magazine* 57 (1930): 160–83.

Servanzi Collio 1838 Servanzi Collio, Severino. "Visita fatta nelli giorni 18 e 19 febrajo 1838 di alcuni oggetti di arte esistenti in Sanseverino dal professor Giovanni Gaye Prussiano in compagnia di me S.S.C." In *Appunti sugli oggetti d'arte nelle chiese di Sanseverino e sua Diocesi*. Ms. n. B4, 1838. Biblioteca Servanzi, San Severino Marche.

Sigmaringen 1875 "Ankäufe für das Museum in Sigmaringen." *Beiblatt zur Zeitschrift für Bildende Kunst*, January 29, 1875, 246–47.

Silver 2020 Silver, Nathaniel. "'Magna ars de talibus tabulis et figuris': Reframing Panel Painting as Venetian Commodity (14th–15th Centuries)." In *Typical Venice? The Art of Commodities, 13th–16th Centuries*, edited by Ella Beaucamp and Philippe Cordez, 69–85. Turnhout, 2020.

***Sitzungsberichte* 1868** *Sitzungsberichte des Münchener Alterthums-Vereins*. Munich, 1868.

Squadroni 1981 Squadroni, Mario. "Notizie e guida al fondo archivistico di casa Silvestri." *Bollettino della Deputazione di Storia Patria per l'Umbria* 78 (1981): 297–322.

Testi 1909 Testi, Laudedeo. *La storia della pittura veneziana. Parte prima. Le origini*. Bergamo, 1909.

Valentini 1868 Valentini, Domenico. *Il forestiere in Sanseverino-Marche; ossia, Breve indicazione degli oggetti di belle arti e altre cose notevoli esistenti in detta città*. San Severino Marche, 1868.

Van Marle 1924 Van Marle, Raimond. *The Development of the Italian Schools of Painting*. Vol. 4. The Hague, 1924.

Von Lehner 1883 Von Lehner, Friedrich August. *Fürstlich Hohenzollern'sches Museum zu Sigmaringen: Verzeichniss der Gemälde*. Sigmaringen, 1883.

Zuliani 1989 Zuliani, Fulvio. "Maestro dell'Incoronazione della Vergine." In *Da Giotto al Tardogotico: Dipinti dei Musei Civici di Padova dal Trecento alla prima metà del Quattrocento*, edited by D. Banzato, 77–79. Exh. cat. Padua (Musei Civici). Rome, 1989.

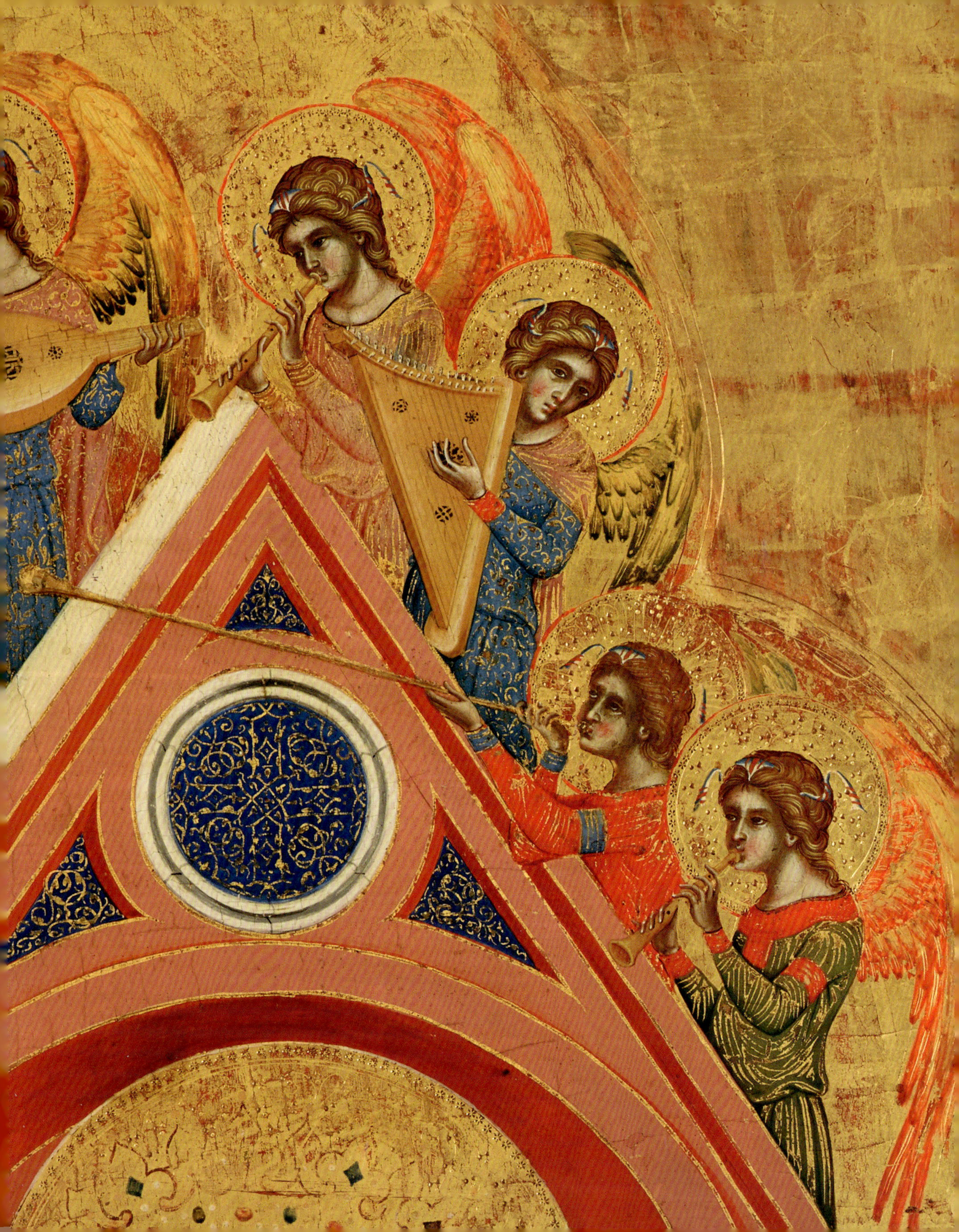

INDEX

Page numbers in *italics* refer to the illustrations.

IMAGE CREDITS

Photographs have been provided by the owners or custodians of the works.
The following list applies to those photographs for which a separate credit is due.

Frontispiece; pp. 6, 10, 18, 68, 73, 78; fig. 1: Joseph Coscia Jr.

Fig. 2: © Wallace Collection, London, UK / Bridgeman Images

Fig. 3: Cameraphoto Arte, Venice / Art Resource, NY

Fig. 4: akg-images / Cameraphoto

Fig. 5: Musei Civici Vicenza – Museo Civico di Palazzo Chiericati

Figs. 6, 15: © Gallerie dell'Accademia di Venezia / su concessione del Ministero della Cultura

Fig. 7: © Diocesi Patriarcato di Venezia

Fig. 8: © Per gentile concessione della Procuratoria di San Marco, Archivio Fotografico della Procuratoria di San Marco

Figs. 9, 10: Su concessione del Ministero della cultura

Fig. 11: Institute of Art History, Zagreb, Photographic Collection (IPU-F-HU-153)

Fig. 12: Scala / Luciano Romano / Art Resource, NY

Fig. 13: Scala / Art Resource, NY

Fig. 16: © DeA Picture Library / Art Resource, NY

Fig. 17: © Victoria and Albert Museum, London

Figs. 19, 20, 27, 29: Xavier F. Salomon

Fig. 21: Jakob Faurvig © Thorvaldsens Museum

Fig. 22: Reiner Löbe, D-72511 Bingen

Figs. 24, 30: © The Frick Collection / Mauro Magliani

Figs. 32, 33, 34: Illustrations by Joseph Godla for The Frick Collection